BLACK MADNESS :: MAD BLACKNESS

BLACK MADNESS

:: MAD BLACKNESS

THERÍ ALYCE PICKENS   Duke University Press   *Durham and London*   2019

© 2019 Duke University Press
All rights reserved
Printed in the United States of America on acid-free paper ∞
Designed by Courtney Leigh Baker
Typeset in Garamond Premier Pro and Knockout by Copperline Books

Library of Congress Cataloging-in-Publication Data
Names: Pickens, Theri A., author.
Title: Black madness : : mad Blackness / Theri Alyce Pickens.
Description: Durham : Duke University Press, 2019. | Includes
bibliographical references and index.
Identifiers: LCCN 2018040998 (print) | LCCN 2018056886 (ebook)
ISBN 9781478005506 (ebook)
ISBN 9781478003748 (hardcover : alk. paper)
ISBN 9781478004042 (pbk. : alk. paper)
Subjects: LCSH: Minority people with disabilities—United States. |
African Americans with disabilities—United States. | People with
disabilities—United States. | Discrimination against people with
disabilities—United States. | American fiction—African American
authors—History and criticism. | Science fiction, American—
History and criticism. | Race in literature. | People with disabilities
in literature. | African Americans—Study and teaching. | Disability
studies—United States.
Classification: LCC HV1569.3.M55 (ebook) | LCC HV1569.3.M55 P53
2019 (print) | DDC 362.4089/96073—dc23
LC record available at https://lccn.loc.gov/2018040998

Duke University Press gratefully acknowledges the support of the
Roger J. Schmutz Fund at Bates College, which provided funds
toward the publication of this book.

Cover art: Lorna Simpson, *Enumerated*, 2016. Ink and screenprint
on claybord. 36 × 24 × ¾ in. © Lorna Simpson. Courtesy the artist
and Hauser & Wirth.

For the **MAD BLACK** *and* **BLACK MAD** *everywhere*

CONTENTS

PREFACE OR ABOUT FACE, GIVING FACE

So my "method," to use a new "lit. crit." word, is not fixed but relates to what I read and the historical context of the writers I read and to the many critical activities in which I am engaged, which may or may not involve writing. It is a learning from the language of creative writers, which is one of surprise, so that I might discover what language I might use.
—BARBARA CHRISTIAN, "The Race for Theory"

Call it the taint—as in
T'aint one and t'aint the other—
illicit and yet naming still
what is between.
—NATASHA TRETHEWEY, "The Book of Castas," *Thrall*

Let me tell you a secret. My first book, *New Body Politics* (Routledge, 2014), bowed to the exigencies of a traditional intellectual project. It started as an ambitious little dissertation with loosely connected ideas. Like most drafts, it was a large-scale project that felt unwieldy even as I worked because I wasn't sure what intervention I wished to make. Over time, I reshaped it into an argument that was more specific and tailored. I used my Muggle-born intellectual talents to craft it into a traditional monograph: five chapters, a separate introduction, and a clear conclusion. The argument moves in a set of concentric circles from the specific to the broad, desiring to prove a point about how the fragility of the body works within contemporary African American and Arab American literatures.[1] Much like other literary and cultural criticism monographs, I examine primary sources and use secondary and theoretical sources mostly to frame my discussions of the literature. This traditional style serves a very particular purpose in the profession: it demonstrates that I have enough competence in the field to make an argument, and prove it using literature and other cultural artifacts as my source material. Plus, tenure.

I tell you this so-called secret (I mean everyone will know now) and draw attention to the picayune parameters of my project to make a modest point that might comfort some people: this is not the only way to create a book project. Clearly, the second book project can have a different genesis and, as is the case with the one you now hold, an entirely different purpose. For *Black Madness :: Mad Blackness*, my aim is not to trace an idea or prove an argument, but rather to open up two fields to each other. To be honest, I was less curious about (and less interested in) literature as a set of primary sources than as a set of theoretical ones. They speak back to critics. And, if critics do not listen, we (ma)linger in thinking of them as having value because they solely illuminate a topic we have already decided to discuss. What happens when we view them as the drivers of these conversations? What solipsism do we avoid when we view them as theoretical sources that change the conversations critics are already having? This not only alters our engagement with primary sources but also fundamentally changes our relationship to secondary and theoretical sources.

For this reason and this outlook, I would label *Black Madness :: Mad Blackness* deliberately wayward. To be fair, this outlook is not new: I join the tradition of Black feminist scholars who understood their projects would reverberate beyond the strictures of traditional academic or institutional structures.[2] The objects of inquiry here are not a series of primary sources but rather a set of conversations. The literature is there to open up the conversations critics have neglected to have. So, this book is not patterned in a traditional fashion: it does not have five chapters, a separate introduction, and a conclusion. The topic, Blackness and madness, does not allow it. Although one might push through an introduction—provide some degree of orientation—concluding becomes an impossibility. No one can end a discussion about intertwined Blackness and madness neatly, if at all. I have chosen not to. I have also deliberately placed an image at the end of the project that serves as a second cover. It is a provocation: a gesture that there is more room to explore, possibly another beginning. In addition, the work often buried in footnotes or hidden by the invocation of a scholar or phrase has sometimes been laid open. At times, awkwardly so. I meander with these critical conversations so that someone can think alongside me. The kind of organization and clarity demanded by my subject matter may not be familiar. Dear reader, you may have to learn to think madly. Blackly.

Footnotes and epigraphs operate here with my particular kind of scholarly quirk. I use them in this writing similarly to how I have used them before in that I expect them to do a substantive amount of work in pushing the conversation beyond the four walls of this text.[3] Often, as critics, we are disciplined to read and write such that we bury the labor of research and conversation in the footnotes and privilege our own voices in the prose. While this strategy is useful for presenting a more traditional argument, my wayward project here requires that the footnotes and epigraphs differently participate in and shape the conversation of which they are a part. I chose my epigraphs from Black women's poetry since they push the debates in new directions, hint at possibilities, when and where I enter. The footnotes are not solely explanations of sources and methodologies, but they also signify, joke, pun, turn a phrase, explore. Both the footnotes and epigraphs are asides, witticisms, and musings. They expose how certain voices and ideas move through my work here and could, later, move through another scholar's. I invite you to theorize from above and below.

I am profoundly guided by a distrust of linearity. The progressive linear narrative seeks to make neat and orderly a set of events and ideas that are messy by design. From a pedagogical standpoint, the linear narrative is useful since it helps us create and impart a story about how we think. Nonetheless, I find it ungenerous for my particular pedagogy here. To teach myself (and perhaps others?) how to think differently means that linear narratives about our work in Blackness and madness have to become unstable. Within this monograph, the result is that the conversations (what are elsewhere called chapters) could feasibly flow from one to another (echoing the tracing or mapping desires of a traditional monograph), but they also could (should?) be read as overlapping discussions. They refer back to each other, revise, augment, and, sometimes, may contradict. This still serves the primary function of this book: to get us to think about how we think when we think about Blackness and madness. In terms of method, this allows my project to abide in, foster, and participate in the kind of messiness that a study of Blackness and madness requires. For that reason, Barbara Christian's words function not only as epigraph but incantation. Of her own method, she writes that it is "not fixed but relates to what I read and the historical context of the writers I read and to the many critical activities in which I am engaged, which may or may not involve writing. It is a learning from the language of creative writers, which is one of surprise, so that I might discover what language I might use."[4] The skepticism about linearity here reverberates as a suspicion about language itself such that I refuse to trust the stories we've heretofore told about Blackness and madness. This book looks for the surprise.

When reflecting on this particular book project, I would be remiss if I did not acknowledge the relative privilege in which it was crafted. I started this project prior to tenure, but finished it after. The freedom to write what you wish at the pace you need exponentially increases after securing the stability tenure provides. I undertook this project feeling battle weary and cynical about the mere possibilities of writing and researching Blackness and madness, especially in a geopolitical space architected by hatred of those two identity categories (among others). I understand my own precarity—in raced, abled, and gendered terms—too acutely to ignore how it expands and constricts my work. And, yet, the freedom to write and think allowed for a set of experiments that permit me to expansively explore what it means to be Black and mad. This is at the crux of the conversations that follow: the contradictory and all too common conundrum of existing at the interstices, intersections, and, still, the margins. Here, Natasha Trethewey's poetry echoes, also as incantation. This is the taint: the putatively unwanted, forgotten, ignored, or ugly space out of which something else can emerge. It is not one and not the other. Quite literally, the "not." And, yet, it also exists as a space of beauty and darkness all its own. To name it, "call it the taint,"[5] knowing it is illicit, strikes me as the primary conceit of this project: I name and call and write in the spirit of discussing not only what remains taboo but also pressing us to discuss it in ways that disrupt how we avoid the subject. Taint one. Taint the other.

I am humbled daily by my faith walk, the overwhelming love of the cross. I would rather have splinters near the foot of Calvary than smooth hands standing on my own. I am grateful for those who cared about me while I cared about this project. I write their names here as acknowledgment, knowing that mere mention does not suffice as thanks. Some people are mentioned more than once because they filled multiple roles. I apologize for any oversights.

I am thankful that I was able to complete this project within a supportive environment. I appreciate my colleagues in the Bates College English Department: Christina Malcolmson, Jessica Anthony, José Villagrana, Lillian Nayder, Robert Farnsworth, Robert Strong, Sanford Freedman, Steven Dillon, Sylvia Federico, Tiffany Salter, Timothy Lyle, and Eden Osucha.

Thank you to those among the Bates faculty (past and present) who took the time to be adroit intellectual interlocutors and/or lend a kind word throughout this process: Adriana Salerno, Aleksandar Diamond-Stanic, Alero Akporiaye, Alexandre Dauge-Roth, Ali Akhtar, Amy Bradfield Douglass, Andrew Baker, Áslaug Ásgeirsdóttir, Baltasar Fra-Molinero, Carol Dilley, Carolina Gonzalez Valencia, Caroline Shaw, Charles "Val" Carnegie, Charles Nero, Dale Chapman, Daniel Riera-Crichton, David Cummiskey, Donald Dearborn, Elizabeth Eames, Emily Kane, Erica Rand, Francesco Duina, Heidi Taylor, Helen Boucher, Hilmar Jensen, James "Jim" Parakilas, James "Jim" Richter, Jason Castro, John Baughman, Joseph Hall, Joshua Rubin, K. Ian Shin, Kathryn "Kathy" Low, Lauren Ashwell, Laurie O'Higgins, Leslie Hill, Lisa Maurizio, Mara Casey Tieken, Marcus Bruce, Margaret Imber, Melinda Plastas, Meredith Greer, Nancy Koven, Nathan Lundblad, Patrick Otim, Paula Schlax, Peter Wong, Rachel Boggia, Rebecca Herzig, Stephanie Kelley-Romano, Steven Engel, Sue E. Houchins, Thomas Tracy, Travis Gould, and Yinxing "Mia" Liu.

The wonderful staff here has done the significant detailed work that keeps life running smoothly. Thank you to Alison Keegan, Christine Schwartz (and all the dining services staff), Denise Begin, Laura Wardwell, Lori Ouellette, Kelly Perreault, and the folks in Facilities Management. I could not have done this without the tireless dedication of my student assistants: Akinyele Akinruntan, John "Jack" Kay, Katherine Blandford, Kathryn Ailes, Leigh Michael, Nicole Kanu, Quincy Snellings, Rebecca Salzman Fiske, and Robert "RJ" Bingham.

There is no way to complete a book project without people who take on the arduous task of reading and commenting on your work. I deeply appreciate how much time and energy that took. I hope that you are all repaid one-hundred-million-fold. Thank you to my sister scholars writing group: Aisha Lockridge, Andreá N. Williams, Ayesha Hardison, Courtney Marshall, Kameelah Martin, and Leslie Wingard. I also extend my heartfelt gratitude to Alison Kafer, Christina Sharpe, Courtney Baker, Erica Rand, Margaret Price, Michael Bérubé, Sharon P. Holland, Stephanie Kerschbaum, and Rebecca Herzig. Your sacrifice of time and energy buoyed me.

A special thank you to those who kept me accountable for doing this work. You all inspire me into sitting each day (save the weekend!) and finding joy in the doing. I am amazed and excited to be in intellectual community with you: Andie Reid, Angela Ards, Ann Marie Russell, Anna Mollow, Ayana Jameison, Brandon Manning, Brian Purnell, Brittney Cooper, C. Riley Snorton, Candice Jenkins, Carol Fadda, Cassandra Jones, Charlotte Karem Albrecht, Chinyere Osuji, Christopher Freeburg, Cynthia "Cindy" Wu, Deborah Vargas, Dennis Britton, Dennis Tyler Jr., Donna Besch, Earl Brooks, Erica Edwards, Ernest J. Mitchell II, Ester Trujillo, Evelyn Alsultany, Evie Shockley, Gene Jarrett, Hayan Charara, Herman Beavers, Howard Rambsy II, Imani Perry, Jacqueline Couti, Jennifer James, John I. Jennings, Jonathan Walton, Joshua Bennett, Judith Casselberry, Kai Green, Kelly Motley, Kelvin Black, Kinohi Nishikawa, Koritha Mitchell, La Marr Jurelle Bruce, LaMonda Stallings, Leila Ben-Nasr, Leon Hilton, Lerone Martin, Liat Ben-Moshe, Mark Anthony Neal, Mejdulene Shomali, Meta DuEwa Jones, Michael Gill, Michelle Wright, Moya Bailey, Nirmala Erevelles, P. Gabrielle Foreman, Penelope K. Hardy, Phil Metres, Randa Jarrar, Rashida Braggs, Reginald Wilburn, Robin D. G. Kelley, Sami Schalk, Stacie McCormick, Stephanie Kerschbaum, Steven Salaita, Susan Burch, Terry Rowden, Tess Chakkalakal, Vivian Lanzot, and Yomaira Figueroa. Special thanks to Richard Yarborough whose indefatigable care as dissertation advisor-turned-colleague (hard to do) allowed me to trust myself in the archive. I am also grateful to the staff at the Huntington Library and Botanical Gardens for their wonderful assistance.

As a disabled person, I move through the world differently, and I know my life would be different and my work would be less than what it is without the help of my medical team. I appreciate you deeply: Deborah Taylor, Reza Rahbar, Katarina Latkovich, and Mitchell Ross of Central Maine Medical Center; Reza Seyedsadjadi, Amanda Guidon, and the rest of the Neurology staff at Massachusetts General Hospital; and all the nurses and pharmacists in Central Maine Medical Center's Oncology and Radiation Center. Toward the tail end of this project, I experienced an intense and protracted medical situation. I extend my heartfelt thanks to those who accompanied me along that journey in Central Maine Medical Center and in Central Maine Medical Center's Rehabilitation Facility, especially Claudia Geyer, Chris York, Deanna Pickard, Elizabeth "Liz" Nadeau, James "Jim" Emond, Jocelyn Murphy, Kathryn "Caddie" Crocker, Kim Wilcox, Lauren F., Leisa Healy, Lisa Mathieu, Nicole Boutaugh, Scott Cyr, Tom Hughes, and ZamZam Mohamud, and a special thanks to my wound warriors: Gisele M. Castonguay for her warmth, wisdom, and wit; and Joanna Norton for being consistently calming, chuckling, and creative. You're Xena and

Gabrielle. Which is which? Depends on the day. Truly, I could not have done this without you.

My dear fr-amily! Where would I be without your laughter, your gentle nudging, your food (!), your beauty. You made this process enjoyable. You help me slay and serve survivor fish. Thank you to Aaisha Tracy, Mara Casey Tieken, Timothy S. Lyle, Sue E. Houchins, Baltasar Fra-Molinero, Charles Nero, Carlos Fra-Nero, Bernardo Fra-Nero, Shanna Benjamin, Leila Pazargadi, Brandon Manning, Nikki Brown, Peyton Cyd Scott, Rob Azubuike, Charif Shanahan, Miriam Petty, Bethel Kifle, Jamil Drake, Muriel Drake, Mariah Drake, Nya Drake, Autumn Drake, Andrea Breau, Shaad Masood, Eidie Breau-Masood, Lauren Breau, Chris Robley, Esmé Breau-Robley, Craig Saddlemire, Julia Harper, Mary Carroll-Robertson, Steven Beaudette, Karen Lane, and Alicia Bonaparte.

My mother, Lori Scott-Pickens, has lived with this project's and my mad Blackness :: Black madness with a generous spirit, a keen wit, more than a little patience, and a little mad Black :: Black mad of her own. There are no satisfactory words to thank you, Mom.

::in my best Missy Elliott voice:: This. Is. A. Ken. Wissoker. Production. I am so proud to have been able to work with you. Thank you for ushering this through thoughtful and detailed reviews and trusting me to work on it at my needed pace. I'm so glad you saw the potential for what this could be. Thank you to the anonymous reviewers who dedicated their time and effort to this project. Warmest gratitude to those who kept the trains running on time at Duke University Press, including Maryam Arain, Jade Brooks, and Olivia Polk. I extend my deepest thanks to Sara Leone, Ivo Fravashi, and everyone who performed copyediting, indexing, and proofreading on this manuscript. Your labor is much appreciated!

This project was generously supported by the Woodrow Wilson Career Enhancement Fellowship, Bates College Faculty Development Fund, and the Whiting Fellowship. Permissions have been granted to use the following epigraphs and artwork: (1) Excerpt from "The Book of Castas" from *Thrall* by Natasha Trethewey. Copyright © 2012 by Natasha Trethewey. Reprinted by permission of Houghton Mifflin Harcourt Publishing Company. All rights reserved. (2) "Sleeping with the Dictionary" from *Sleeping with the Dictionary* by Harryette Mullen © 2002 by the Regents of the University of California. Published by UC Press. (3) "Black Peculiar :: Energy Complex" from *Black Peculiar* by Khadijah Queen © 2011. Published by Noemi Press. (4) "clare's song" from *the new black* © 2011 by Evie Shockley. Published by Wesleyan University Press. (5) Finney, Nikky. "Segregation, Forever." In *Head Off and Split*. Evanston, IL: TriQuarterly Books/Northwestern University Press, 2011. Copyright © 2011 by Nikky Finney. Published 2011 by TriQuarterly Books/Northwestern University Press. All rights reserved. (6) "Flight of the California Condor" from *Imagoes* by Wanda Coleman. Copyright © 1983 by Wanda Coleman. Reprinted by permission of Black Sparrow Press, an Imprint of David R. Godine, Publisher. (7) "The Book of Negroes" from *There Are More Beautiful Things than Beyoncé* by Morgan Parker © 2017. Published by Tin House Books. (8) Wangechi Mutu, *Riding Death in My Sleep, 2002*, Ink and collage on paper, 60 × 44 in., Courtesy of the Artist and Peter Norton.

I beg to dicker with my silver-tongued companion, whose lips are ready to read my shining gloss. A versatile partner, conversant and well-versed in the verbal art, the dictionary is not averse to the solitary habits of the curiously wide-awake reader. In the dark night's insomnia, the book is a stimulating sedative, awakening my tired imagination to the hypnagogic trance of language. —HARRYETTE MULLEN, "Sleeping with the Dictionary," *Sleeping with the Dictionary*

Let's start with a comparative analysis that does not work.

In Leonard Kriegel's autoethnographical essay "Uncle Tom and Tiny Tim: Some Reflections on the Cripple as Negro" (1969), he declares, "Uncle Tom and Tiny Tim are brothers under the skin."[1] Using what he terms a "functional analogy" to Blackness, Kriegel traces his experiences in New York City as a so-called cripple, building a case for equal treatment socioculturally as well as under the law.[2] He links the mandate that disabled people request police escorts to their destinations (suggested by former New York City mayor John Lindsay) to calling a Black man "boy" in a white crowd. Kriegel uses Frantz Fanon as an epigraph and as an interlocutor throughout to critique the injustices he experiences, asserting that Blackness is both "analogy and method" even if the two are, according to him, not something Black America "can yet give itself."[3] In addition to these analogies, Kriegel offers explanatory glosses of his life that speak to living within and internalizing ableism: He feels as though his existence causes his mother pain. He calls his condition a public embarrassment. Within rehabilitation facilities,

he strives to be fixed. At no point does Kriegel discuss a community of similarly (disabled) embodied people, even though he lives in the rehabilitation
facility. The message is plain: being a cripple is bad, and it is just like, if not
worse than, being a Negro.

Quite frankly, Kriegel's essay is painful to read. The outdated language, the
faulty analogy, the internalized ableism, the profound lack of community—
all of these depict experiences of disability and Blackness detached from
social and/or political context. In Kriegel's essay, Blackness and Black social
movements provide a loose social mooring. To write at the tail end of the
1960s in New York requires an engagement with Blackness as a matter of
accuracy and rigor. So, Kriegel's essay considers—as it should—the import
of social positioning vis-à-vis Blackness. Thinking of the essay as an artifact,
it clarifies how the Black power movements and civil rights gains of the 1950s
and 1960s paved the way for disability activism around the Rehabilitation
Act (1973), and, by extension, the Americans with Disabilities Act (1990),
among others. Frantz Fanon provides the essay's central theoretical interlocutor, which could potentially position the "like race" idea less as analogy,
shifting the discursive terrain such that the essay centralizes the projected
experiences of Blackness. It doesn't. Fanon's theories do prove useful, however, in thinking about the social situations that difference creates and abets.

Even though the essay references the world, it is not grounded in it. As a
result, the analysis fails on a few registers. The "like race" analogies for disability function as missed opportunities for nuance. There are only certain
well-worn paths that logic can follow. First, the comparative element leaves
Kriegel little choice but to think through the relationship in hierarchical
terms where one identity is more or less disenfranchised than the other. Indeed, this vacillates for Kriegel depending on the situation (i.e., the disabled
have less social options, but Blacks have been victimized more), which demonstrates a kind of sophistication in understanding that each identity category operates differently depending on social context. Yet, the analogy still
facilitates racist erasure: despite the fact that Kriegel's rehabilitation facility
is in Harlem, he does not think through the life of the Black disabled person, nor does he speculate about the interiority of those around him. They
are merely sullen. The "as" of the simile and, by extension, the "like" of the
larger analogy elide the differences between these identities because rhetorically one replaces the other. Erasure then allows for a collapse of important
distinctions in experience (i.e., difference between Kriegel's European immigrant mother and the Blacks in Harlem), and the depiction of Blackness

as an abject monolith incapable of providing its own analogy and method. Placing Fanon in this context only allows him to expose and explain Blackness as a pathology of the West, rather than allow Fanon to function as a theoretician that dialogues with and about Blackness and disability (albeit one who makes certain problematic "like race" analogies himself). In its failure, Kriegel's essay foregrounds why the "like race" analogies are missed opportunities: They potentially promise a useful engagement with Blackness and disability because they grant that the two share social similarities. However, without addressing collective histories, theoretical impulses, and subjectivities with nuance, the analogy reinscribes the erasure it originally promises to rectify.

Although Kriegel's essay was published in 1969, the theoretical and methodological residues of his project remain. To think through the relationship between race and disability requires answering several questions: How might we read race and disability outside the confines of the scripts heretofore provided? In what ways do we need to shift or challenge existing analytical paradigms? To what aesthetic practices and thinkers do we need to turn to expand our imaginations vis-à-vis these two discourses and material realities? What sacred cows or shibboleths do we need to leave behind methodologically, theoretically, aesthetically?

This project, *Black Madness :: Mad Blackness*, turns to madness and Blackness to answer these questions about race and disability more broadly. Critical discourses about madness and Blackness tend to implicate but not include each other.[4] As a consequence, the criticism recapitulates several pervasive but incomplete ideas. One of those is the loose rendering of Blackness and madness as analogous to each other. More often, the two discourses are examined as extensions of one another, too slippery to parse, yet so inseparable that one can elide or replace the other. In contrast, I theorize that madness (broadly defined) and Blackness have a complex constellation of relationships. These relationships between Blackness and madness (and race and disability more generally) are constituted within the fissures, breaks, and gaps in critical and literary texts. Black madness and mad Blackness then are not interchangeable or reciprocal. Rather, they foreground the multiple and, at times, conflicting epistemological and ontological positions at stake when reading the two alongside each other. In exploring these critical possibilities, I explicate how this set of relationships has, makes, and acquires meaning in the various spaces they occupy without necessarily guaranteeing emancipation or radicality. I turn to what may be an unlikely site to explore:

Black speculative fiction. These artists-theorists disrupt Western epistemology such that their work becomes a locus for thinking through putatively

Explanation for the title!
• Mad studies → activism
• Blackness often disregard-
d in disability studies

Three Words

e as an inroad to describing our current critical moment.[6] *Black Madness :: Mad Blackness* rests on the idea that ability and race are intertwined, as Michelle Jarman notes, "two dynamic discursive processes that inform one another."[7] Suturing madness and Blackness together, I debunk the perception that the title is redundant, oxymoronic, or excessive. In an ideological construct of white supremacy, Blackness is considered synonymous with madness or the prerequisite for creating madness. To push them together syntactically runs the risk of appearing repetitive, but it also prompts the possibility that the two must be parsed.

Despite my academic and personal proclivity for politesse and rigorous specificity, I choose to rest in the vagueness and insult mad brings.[8] I mobilize this word as part of my critical armature because this discussion requires a direct engagement with slippery and insulting language.[9] Mad carries a lexical range that includes (in)sanity, cognitive disability, anger, and, for anyone who remembers the slang of the 1990s, excess (usually synonymous with too or really). In common parlance, it is used pejoratively and remains rather vague. However, mad studies takes up madness to "represent a critical alternative to 'mental illness' or 'disorder' as a way of naming and responding to emotional, spiritual, and neuro-diversity."[10] Mad studies perspectives mobilize activist and scholastic impulses in their refusal of the historical definitions of madness as "irrationality, a condition involving decline or even disappearance of the role of rational factor in the organization of human conduct and experience" and the equation of madness with lack or inability.[11] In this field, the biopsychiatric definitions of madness that proceed from this historical definition—wedded to inability and irrationality—no longer hold since they disenfranchise the perspectives of those harmed by psy-disciplines. In this study, I take seriously the critical impulses of mad studies: I keep a tension between psychosocial definitions of madness (without attributing causality) and biomedical definitions (without attributing authority), while resisting an uncritical celebration of madness as experience or as metaphor. Even though this project focuses on those who would be labeled mad or embrace being mad, I also do not veer too far away from the critical possibilities of madness as a "slippery and unruly object."[12] When madness does not solely refer to the experience of a mad person but rather pans outward as a larger discourse, it challenges how "the psychic, cognitive, and affective dimensions of experience are parceled out into categories . . . all under the supposedly 'empirical' authority of medical science and psychiatric expertise as much as through the exercise of legal and juridical power."[13] In other words, it is everywhere and affects everything. Maddeningly so.

In *Black Madness :: Mad Blackness*, Black functions as a racial category, cultural affiliation, and social position. I use Black for its lexical and sociocultural range. It includes a wide variety of people and experiences within the diaspora and does not limit the discussion to a specific geopolitical imaginative space. Unfortunately, my discussion is limited in scope to the parts of the diaspora that share an intellectual inheritance with North America and Europe. As Julie Livingston's *Debility and the Moral Imagination in Botswana* (2005) and Nirmala Erevelles's *Disability and Difference in Global Contexts* (2011) make clear, definitions of Blackness and disability cannot and should not be moved carelessly across transnational borders.[14] Yet, given the vastness of colonial and imperial projects where race determines life and death, the study of Blackness emerges as a fecund space to think through how material consequences manifest. As I have claimed elsewhere, a turn to Blackness "authorizes a reconceptualization of history, culture, and politics" if the field is understood as "a set of traditions, reading practices, and valuation systems operating alongside, intertwined with, but also independent from those of whiteness."[15] Like madness, Blackness is also everywhere and affects everything. It is my hope that despite the necessary geopolitical limitations of my project, it later proves useful for those studying other Blacknesses.

I choose to nominalize Black and mad by adding the suffix "ness" to attend to the two words as both description and category. I bring them together grammatically to theorize about the constellation of relationships that comprise the two. Nirmala Erevelles, in writing about the Middle Passage, rereads Hortense Spillers's work to point out that the simplified causal relationship—slavery produces disability—does not fully encompass the way disability and Blackness function. Rather, "disability/impairment and race are neither merely biological nor wholly discursive, but rather are historical material constructs imbricated within the exploitative conditions of transnational capitalism."[16] My staged grammatical intervention in the title calls attention to how a revision of this sort works. It is at once a reference to the material conditions and consequences as well as a discursive attending to the categories' imbrication. Nominalizing the two also staves off what Rachel Gorman argues is "the mad subject . . . constituted as the white subject at the horizon of whiteness"[17]: that is, the mad white subject who can be embraced by whiteness through a discourse of universality. In this formulation, Blackness modifies (and I use the grammatical term deliberately) who and what is mad. Madness as noun calls attention to what Sami Schalk insists is a useful slippage between materiality and metaphor in Black studies. She argues that within Black literature, disability takes on "concrete and metaphorical meanings" such that disability can "symbolize something other than disability while still being about disability." In so doing, "disability metaphors therefore allow us to explore the historical and material connections between disability and other social systems of privilege and oppression."[18] As with Erevelles's formulation, the two categories do not exist in a simple causal or analogic relationship; they inform each other such that madness modifies how we understand Blackness.[19]

The third putative word of the title, the double colon, teases and disrupts. The title signals that there are differences between Black madness and mad Blackness but one is not an analogy for the other, nor does one explain the other, nor does one cause the other. Although the double colon tends to stand for analogy, the use of it here does not affirm that the two are such, but rather questions the grammars and assumptions that lie dormant in thinking of them as analogous (a query I highlight by calling the double colon a word above). I toy with the double colon as a convention of the academic project specifically because what typically follows the colon is supposed to explicate or clarify. In this case, the so-called clarification is meant to unsettle. The double colon also nods to the tradition of Black speculative fiction on which this project focuses. In the introduction to *Afro-Future Females: Black Writers Chart Science Fiction's Newest New-Wave Trajectory* (2008), Marleen Barr claims, "A period printed on a page resembles a planet backgrounded by white space vastness."[20] Whereas Barr usefully thinks of the period as a manifestation of Black/white encounter in science fiction authorship, I find the period-as-planet evocative for how it forces a more expansive understanding of that which we once thought of as finite. Again, the causal, analogic, and explicative relationships do not fully capture how Black and mad function together. Instead, the four period/planets of the double colon invite us to think of them as more vast in scope than heretofore imagined.[21]

As my explication of the title suggests, this project brings the conversations within disability studies and critical race studies together somewhat uneasily without positioning either as emancipatory vis-à-vis the other. Since disability studies, as a field, borrows heavily from the gains of critical race studies and women's studies, race is always already embedded in scholastic discussions of disability. However, the principles of critical race studies tend to have a penumbral presence because disability studies rarely engages whiteness as a social position and often thinks of Blackness as a contribution rather than part of its construction.[22] As long as whiteness remains the normative racial category, investigations of disability that do not address whiteness directly leave open crucial lacunae. In *Disability Theory* (2008), Tobin Siebers brings to bear the advances of critical race theory to disability theory as a way to formulate a complex understanding of how identity theories work, contingent as they all are on what he terms "the ideology of ability."[23] I agree that a commitment to and desire for ability undergirds common praxis, but Siebers misses an opportunity to examine how the presumption of ability accompanies whiteness and how much such a presumption undergirds disability theory and scholarship (I take this up in greater detail in the third conversation). Likewise, Lennard Davis's *End of Normal* (2014) speculates that now diversity does the semantic and cultural heavy lifting that normal used to perform as he rethinks the accepted wisdom on topics as varied as Freud and end-of-life decisions. Yet, as compelling as Davis's work is on these subjects, it takes as its premise that we have moved beyond identity.[24] Lurking within this logic is the same rhetorical movement performed by Nietzsche: as soon as decolonization opened up the space for those who had been objects of history to assert themselves as subjects, subjects faced their theoretical death. We have not moved beyond identity because we have not moved beyond whiteness as a standard, invisibilized though it may be. Here, Alison Kafer's questions about the future of disability studies, methodological inclusion, and theoretical impulse become particularly instructive: "In which theories and in which movements do we recognize ourselves, or recognize disability, and which theories and movements do we continue to see as separate from or tangential to disability studies?"[25]

One such opportunity for the future of disability studies lies in its inclusion of madness. In what some scholars term a twist of irony, disability studies "forged as it has been with physical impairment as its primary terrain, has inherited damaging ableist assumptions of 'mind.'"[26] I concur that in the field of disability studies, "physical disability stands in for disability *in* lectual disability is more readily and widely ...... anization than is physical disability."[27] For ...... the future of disability studies must include scholars of rhetoric who are at the forefront of work on intellectual disability with their explorations of autism, neuroatypicality, and mental illness.[28] *Black Madness :: Mad Blackness* opens up the opportunity to examine how the charges of cognitive disability and mental illness (i.e., *drapetomania* as a mental illness causing Black slaves to run away) or congenital, race-based neuroatypicality (i.e., all Blacks are mentally deficient) bear repercussions for imagining, analyzing, and theorizing Blackness and madness.[29] As mentioned before, madness remains slippery, as both real and imagined, claimed and refused. What remains stable is that madness is understood as a function of language, one with which disability studies must engage as text. Following the logic of Tanya Titchkosky in *Reading and Writing Disability Differently* (2007), we must begin to read madness as a text in our studies, since "claiming to know disability, while not experiencing a need to reflect upon the assumptions, organization and consequences of this knowledge is a common yet potentially oppressive social practice."[30] I would add that it is definitely an oppressive scholastic practice if we choose not to reflect on how our intellectual enterprise is upheld by sanist notions of mind.

Thus far, critical work, including my own, about Blackness and disability has, like disability studies generally, focused on physical disability and chronic illness. For those scholars situated in or claimed by disability studies, the discussions of Blackness and disability have been illegible because they challenge certain academic conventions. For instance, Christopher M. Bell's edited collection *Blackness and Disability: Critical Examinations and Cultural Interventions* (2011) functions as one of the inaugural moments of Black disability studies (more in the first conversation), since it sought to shift the conversation in African American studies from being ableist and the conversation in disability studies from being "concerned with white bodies."[31] The collection includes scholars whose citational praxis does not always make use of well-known disability studies scholars or whose work does not necessarily include the word disability. To my mind, what appears to be a set of mistakes actually reveals that when Blackness and disability cohere, they challenge each other institutionally and allow for the possibility that disability or race may be called by other names. As with the language of madness, no language regarding disability is neutral, which means that the euphemisms in common parlance (i.e., the sugar for diabetes, or touched for cognitively disabled) make their way into critical literature differently as well (i.e., health care discrepancies and differentials in treatment for diabetes, or discussions about outsiders within a family/community). What appears to be a gap in this discussion of race and disability actually requires a rereading of the critical literature, since in Black cultural and critical contexts, disability is often operating in other registers. As mentioned in the preface, one has to think Blackly or madly. Tamika L. Carey, in *Rhetorical Healing: The Reeducation of Contemporary Black Womanhood* (2016), links the discourse of healing and wellness to Black women's literacy of their environment. Disability—as a set of social and cultural practices—subtends Carey's discussion when she elaborates on Black women's writing as a set of "talking and reading cures" that allow them to detail the complexities of racism and sexism.[32] Far from considering disability auxiliary or merely part of an overcoming narrative, Carey's articulation of wellness allows disability to be the vector through which some of the Black women writers in her study articulate their encounters with misogynoir. One of the other registers at stake is erasure: Rebecca Wanzo's *The Suffering Will Not Be Televised* (2009) explores how Black women's suffering, because of an American obsession with sentimentality in narrative, remains illegible to a larger public Here, disability functions as a social structure that by virtue of ableist reliance on pity and sympathy determines who gets to belong to the category disabled and whose experience of illness can be validated in the public sphere. Recent projects, including the fiftieth anniversary special issue of *African American Review* on Blackness and disability (just to name one), have attempted to rectify these lacunae, push against the invisibility of race by proposing new methodologies (e.g., Christopher M. Bell's representational detective work, Sami Schalk's emphasis on materiality in metaphor, Leon Hilton's theorization of wandering, Anna Mollow's schema of fat Black disability studies), mining historiographical gaps (e.g., Douglas Baynton's exploration of civil rights discourse, Dea Boster's analysis of slavery, Michael Gill and Nirmala Erevelles's rereading of Henrietta and Elsie Lacks), performing hermeneutical readings of various texts (e.g., Jeffrey Brune's archival work on John Howard Griffin, Timothy S. Lyle's interrogation of pleasure in Pearl Cleage, Dennis Tyler Jr.'s staged conversation between James Weldon Johnson's fiction and autobiography, Sarah Orem's readings of Black disaster in *Grey's Anatomy*), or pushing against national boundaries (e.g., Julie Livingston's exploration of Botswana, Claire Barker's emphasis on postcolonial literature).

I choose to name these scholars explicitly as part of a scholarly politic that lays bare what work has already been done and by whom so that we can no longer remark that the two fields do not speak to each other. Moreover, unearthing where disability appears in Black studies and where Blackness appears in disability studies scholarship bolsters one of the main contentions of *Black Madness :: Mad Blackness*. There exists a wide constellation of critical relationships between Blackness and disability writ large, and Blackness and madness in particular. Mining landmark scholarship in Black studies bears this out. For example, Valerie Smith's discussion of the garret space in *Incidents in the Life of a Slave Girl*, in addition to being a crucial study for Black feminist thought, positions the architecture of confinement and therefore that which creates disability as preferable to the conditions of slavery and enabling freedom.[33] Neither Smith's work nor the text under scrutiny explicitly heralds disability as radical, but each makes that potential clear. Henry Louis Gates Jr.'s concept of the "talking book" assumes a wide variety of possibilities for communication that includes double voicing, intertextuality, and silence. To trouble notions of how a text speaks is to allow for the possibility that cognition, communication, and ability upend or cocreate said text. Gates's and Smith's work remains undergirded by the presence of disability even if it is not explicitly acknowledged and called as such. Disability does appear explicitly in some texts, such as Alice Walker's meditations on her blindness in "Beauty: When the Other Dancer Is the Self" (1983) and Audre Lorde's essays in *Burst of Light* (1988) and *Cancer Journals* (1980). In the work of the political scientist Cathy J. Cohen, disability surfaces in a discussion of HIV/AIDS. Cohen's *The Boundaries of Blackness: HIV and the Breakdown of Black Politics* (1999) indicts the segments of Black communities that refused to care for the ill and the dying based on narrow definitions of racial identity. Of late, critical race scholars La Marr Jurelle Bruce and Nicole Fleetwood examined the prevalence of disability in discourses surrounding Black celebrities Lauryn Hill and Rihanna, respectively, in a special issue of *African American Review*, edited by Soyica Colbert, on Black performance. They each argue that for these Black women entertainers disability—particularly madness—changes public perception of their voice. For Lauryn Hill, the use of crazy-as-insult makes it permissible to ignore her critiques of the music industry and its exploitation of her. For Rihanna, mobilizing craziness allows her some latitude in her creative and erotic projects. Bruce and Fleetwood's work—limited only because of the genre of the article—focuses on how Blackness mediates the understanding of presumed disability and in some cases facilitates erasure.[34]

Black Madness :: Mad Blackness furthers the conversations above by fore-grounding the spaces where Blackness and madness become usefully en-tangled. My goal, however, is not to unravel them but rather to pinpoint the facets of their intertwining so that we might rest with the knots history and culture have created. This project attempts an intellectual cartography. Invoking Morrison, "I want to draw a map . . . of a critical geography and use that map to open . . . space for discovery, intellectual adventure, and close exploration,"[35] since the ways we've drawn connections and borders between Blackness and madness have heretofore closed off possibilities or rendered them in simplistic terms. In offering a way to read and conceive of Blackness and madness conjoined, this project assumes what most intellectual cartog-raphies have borne out: racism and ableism are quotidian practices in which the experience of being raced and being disabled are mundane. For that rea-son, one cannot have race without disability, nor disability without race. We used to remark often that disability studies has been slow to discuss issues of race and vice versa. As my discussion above has made clear, we should revise that to point out that despite the increased conversations about race and disability generally and madness and Blackness in particular, scholarship tends to tenuously connect the two, and that connection, however critically useful, can be and has been easily severed for reasons of political expediency. This is what happens when Blackness is considered a problem for disability revolution. This is what happens when disability is considered a problem for Black revolution. In what follows, I theorize about the places where and reasons why the relationship between the two refuses to so easily fall apart.

I turn to an unlikely site to discuss Blackness and madness: Black specu-lative fiction. As so many others have already proven, race and ability are historically and materially constructed. So, my recourse to a genre that de-liberately unmoors itself from time and space may seem strange. This un-likely site, what science fiction critic Darko Suvin termed the "literature of cognitive estrangement,"[36] distinguishes itself in its attending to the fact in the fiction.[37] This formulation usefully clarifies how speculative fiction comments on the sanity of the world it inhabits and how that genre attempts to define sanity. However, the idea of "cognitive estrangement" needs some clarification vis-à-vis madness. That is, what does speculative fiction do in its discussion of madness? First, "cognitive estrangement" implies dissonance and distress, but does not imply madness per se. The term cannot stretch to accommodate experiences of madness like those that mad studies takes seriously: those that are patient-centered and skeptical of psy-disciplines, particularly those that allow for or court a narrative resolution. To be clear, this strikes me as a limitation of "cognitive estrangement" as a term, not mad studies as an interdisciplinary enterprise or Black speculative fiction as a literary endeavor. The term madness, my staged grammatical intervention in this project's title and method, helpfully intervenes as a way to prompt a discussion of the fact in the fiction, the strange in the cognitive, the dissonance in the distress, but it does not take for granted that madness will be resolved by the narrative's end.

Second, the understanding of "cognitive estrangement" in speculative fiction has to be situated within a conversation about how race functions in that genre. I concur with Isiah Lavender III's description of the "Blackground" of speculative fiction, the space where the race meanings in the genre become discernible and andré carrington's idea that the creation of speculative fiction ushers in the creations of refracted Blacknesses.[38] For both Lavender and carrington, reading race requires reading against some of the cognition that guides the creative work within this genre. So, if we are to consider that speculative fiction attempts to unsettle how readers think, but typically fails to do so in the area of race, then we must consider how a discussion about race also requires that we shift reading practices. Madness then opens up "cognitive estrangement" to question just exactly how strange cognition about Blackness and madness can be. In other words, Darko Suvin did not know how right he was: we must attend to the facts of Blackness and madness in the (speculative) fiction.

Reading madness and Blackness conjoined in Black speculative fiction indexes the profound possibilities within that genre. Slippages within the genre take for granted multiple forms of cognition, mental engagement, and racial difference such that Black speculative fiction becomes a welcoming place for those who are seeking a way out of their minds. A less tongue-in-cheek, though no less slippery answer lies in one of the premier Black speculative fiction artist-theorist's ruminations on the utility of the genre with regard to theorizing about the world. In Octavia E. Butler's essay "Positive Obsession," she wrote for *Essence* readers a rebuttal to (or a rebuke of) the question "What good is all this [science fiction] for Black people?"[39] She counters the assumption embedded within the question that literature must do something for material conditions. She points out not only that she resents the question but also that the genre "stimulates imagination and creativity," "gets reader and writer off the beaten track," and, in its "examination of the possible effects of science and technology or social organization and political direction," prompts "alternative ways of thinking and doing."[40] More importantly for this discussion, her enumerated answers as well as her rhetorical questions (answers by paraleipsis) suggest that the unmooring of time, space, and culture in science fiction prompts the necessary tumult required to reimagine the world.

Butler (like the rest of the writers that follow—Nalo Hopkinson, Tananarive Due, and Mat Johnson) operates as a theorist in line with Barbara Christian's formulation of theory and narrative, as outlined in "The Race for Theory": namely, their narratives, riddles, proverbs, stories, and fiction are how they theorize in dynamic rather than static forms.[41] Their conversations about time, social location, space, and place invite readers to reexamine how to read Blackness and madness alongside each other. They each scrutinize the monstrous intimacy of the novel,[42] highlighting how it functions as a pedagogic enterprise designed to inculcate and discipline Black bodies with their own erasure. In much of this project, I focus on the way their theorizing manifests in the content of their fiction. It is only at the end of this project that I deliberately turn to a discussion of genre (the novel) itself. These writers participate in a rich tradition of Black speculative fiction that upends the erasure of Blackness in fiction writ large and the dismissal of madness as mere metaphor. At the interstices of a raced and gendered madness, we find the seams of the Enlightenment project. When speculative fiction writers suspend time, space, and culture, they force further apart the disjuncture between what is natural and what is cultural inheritance. Even though the content of the fiction under scrutiny seeks to disentangle itself from time as a particular concept, the fiction remains steeped in discourses that have long histories, including racist antebellum pseudoscience, disability as the rationale against civil rights gains, and rhetoric that binds white racism to a series of unspeakable and unintelligible acts.[43] Yet, their writing does not obscure the tension between systemic racism and ableism, on the one hand, and seemingly individual and singular intimate acts, on the other. What these writers foreground is that it would be willfully naïve to assume white madness as the only rationale for racism or to dismiss how much racism is mundane and so is madness, but the latter is not an excuse or a reason for the former.

To be clear, I do not believe that this project has implications solely for Black speculative fiction (as I discuss in the final conversation). Given the history of literacy and race in the United States, all Black writers are a science fiction come to life. Including me. Given the history of disability and science, many disabled people live in the interstices of science and fiction. Including me. Within the long history of Black literature, madness surfaces not solely as pathology or as part of a holy fool tradition, but also as a viable alternative to engagements with white racism even if it does not result in increased agency. Madness becomes the place to engage because racism adheres to a peculiar kind of rationality, predicated on the long history of the Enlightenment and its material effects. Critical mad studies, when combined with critical race studies, becomes beneficially disruptive as a way to call attention to Black madness as a viable social location from which people have been engaged. From Pauline Hopkins's novel *Of One Blood, Or the Hidden Self* (1902), which might be termed Black speculative fiction, to Angelina Weld Grimké's play *Rachel* (1914) to George Wolfe's play *The Colored Museum* (1986) and others, Black mad characters are everywhere. Their madnesses and their Blacknesses are expansive. Furthermore, the examples of Blackness and madness do not merely exist in fiction. They find their way together into the public sphere and global headlines as examples of what occurs when the full force of delegitimizing power gets marshaled against two social locations whose construction tends to hinge on their relationship to nonnormativity: media discussions of Black rage, the aftermath of state-sanctioned and extrajudicial killings of Black people, and the gaslighting of non-Black allies.[44]

In my methodology, I take for granted that the reading acts that privilege madness and Blackness are participatory. Shoshana Felman and Toni Morrison agree that reading madness and race respectively requires participation in the form of decision-making on the part of the reader.[45] Their understanding of the world must be engaged—in order to be confirmed or disrupted. According to Felman and Morrison, readers must decide which portions of the content they will privilege in their interpretation. Felman's "scandal" that no reader is innocent resonates with Morrison's "playing in the dark," since no reader can be divorced from discussions of race in American letters. To read Blackness and madness then, to participate in such readings, requires that readers bear the responsibility of interpretation: understand that multiple interpretations are available and that their choices indicate a stance on Blackness and madness itself. Since Felman and Morrison's ideas yoke reader response to social, political, and cultural context, they become incredibly useful for thinking through the way mad Blackness and Black madness exceed the boundaries of the text. Indeed, the significant material consequences of each suggest that texts were never meant to hold madness or Blackness. Readerly participation also applies to critical understandings of the two discourses as well. For this reason, each of the conversations in *Black Madness :: Mad Blackness* begins with a discussion of how the critical discourse shapes our engagement. I start there because critics, as readers, are implicated in the scholarly writing about Blackness and madness. Margaret Price's *Mad at School: Rhetorics of Mental Disability and Academic Life* (2011) points this out beautifully by indicating that we are all implicated as scholars in discussions of madness.[46] The professoriate hinges on our ability to pass as sane, or rather the right type of sane.[47] It is the same critique scholars of race have been making for years: to address Blackness/madness imperils the twin pillars of whiteness and sanity that uphold Western notions of intellectual enterprise.

To that end, I draw on those who read within the folds and breaks, a concept and methodology that attends to connections between discourse and materiality as infinite and inextricably bound. The complex web of relationships between Blackness and madness (and race and disability) is constituted within the fissures, breaks, and gaps in critical and literary texts. Hortense Spillers's work in "Interstices: A Drama of Small Words" (1984), and "'Mama's Baby, Papa's Maybe': An American Grammar Book" (1987), opens up this critical space and methodology in her discussion of the flesh. She depicts the flesh as a text that has, makes, and acquires meaning. The flesh of Black women in particular, since it has been erased from history, in its abrogated status exists within what Deleuze later terms the fold: a space not solely of possibility, but one that continuously gets erased. Since Deleuze develops the fold vis-à-vis Leibniz's understanding of the Baroque aesthetic (read: within a tradition of Western and Enlightenment thought), I find it useful to think through how the fold shows up in the aesthetic praxis of the artists-theorists under scrutiny. The fold exists within the self, between the self and other, and between groups of others, as a space from which to interpret and understand the various critical and creative possibilities available. In addition, development does not occur on a linear plane: it constantly folds, unfolds, and refolds. Most important for my readings, the fold functions as a space that creates and sustains possibility. Spillers's work not only anticipates Deleuze but also expands its reach by making explicit which subjects consistently live within the fold, an idea disability studies scholar Lennard Davis echoes when he writes about the way ideas and subjects within the fold get erased.[48] Yet, the fold as understood by Deleuze is not merely the place where history and aesthetics rest. It is mercurial and oppositional, since, as Hortense Spillers theorized prior to Deleuze, it is emblazoned on Black flesh. Fred Moten's *In the Break: The Aesthetics of the Black Radical Tradition* (2003) conceptualizes the "break," a methodological kissing cousin to the fold, as a racialized space that pinpoints how history, music, and race—as discursive concepts and material consequences—function as oppositional even as they are coextensive. Moten's "break" signals the kind of rupture that creates and catastrophizes Blackness and madness, which he punctuates by using other words to describe the break like the cut, or the process of breaking, like invagination, or intussuscepted (all of which I borrow).

In theorizing about the constellation of relationships between Blackness and madness, I find that they have, make, and acquire meaning differently in fiction and critical conversations. For this reason, each discussion makes room for an investigation of the gaps and fissures in critical literature as well as where fiction intervenes. The artists-theorists in this study all challenge the current critical conversations in their dynamic theorizing. My readings of both the critical literature and the fictive text examine the fold (the break, the cut) and the processes that make the fold legible (invagination, intussusception). These ruptures require reading texts countermnemonically with an eye toward gaps and mistakes.[49] I ask pointedly about the way critical conversations are constructed, rehearsed, and furthered. I also ask about where the fiction opens up the possibilities critical conversations have foreclosed. I read within the rupture, the break, the fold, finding the potentials, pitfalls, and the processes of Black madness and mad Blackness. I deliberately stray away from conceptions of Blackness and madness, such as that of Anne Cheng's "racial melancholia," which understands racial identity as beholden to grief, or Paul Gilroy's "postcolonial melancholia," which views history only through the lenses of nostalgia and melancholia.[50] Despite their utility in thinking through the effects of internalized colonialism and racism, melancholia conceptually cannibalizes all other affective engagement and tends to prioritize itself over race, even when the two are supposedly sutured together. To read within these folds points out how Blackness and madness exceed and shift the boundaries and definitions of human, specifically how the assumed subject positions of unknowable excess (that is, Black madness and mad Blackness) jeopardize the neatness with which we draw the line between self and other. Be clear. This is not meant to be an emancipatory theory of agency for Black mad or mad Black subjects. Instead, this project may delineate the costs of hope and the aftermath of degradation.

With good reason, this project pulls from the intellectual activist impulses of both African American studies and disability studies. African American studies as an interdisciplinary field challenges the willful gaps and erasures in other fields, privileging Blackness as a critical analytical category. It is from this impulse of redress and address that I approach disability studies' insistence on the variability of human embodiment and mental ability. I find that the two fields challenge one another to examine points of erasure both inside and outside their own interdisciplinary spaces. They also warn against the commodification of movements by institutions as a proxy for fixing the material conditions of disenfranchised racial minorities and people with disabilities. Though I suture them together, I also seek to parse Blackness from disability, disability from Blackness, since each field has used the discourse of the other to metaphorize its own conditions, even as I take seriously the way both methodologies trouble their relationship to normativity. In this way, my project is indebted to queer studies for its critique of normal as a category, and expansive definitions of familial and erotic attachment. As part of my engagement with these fields, I participate in what Erica Edwards terms "a politics of curiosity" or in Alison Kafer's "unanswered questions and contradictions" that seek to open up new, if fraught, intellectual terroir.[51]

Because of my emphasis on the processes and potentials of Blackness and madness together, I choose to read the two through the lens of intersectionality. This particular theoretical approach—described as such by Kimberlé Crenshaw and theorized well before her[52]—relies on the interrelated nature of identity as formation and lived experience. I harness the motility associated with Crenshaw's idea of the intersection. In "Demarginalizing the Intersection of Race and Sex: A Black Feminist Critique of Antidiscrimination Doctrine, Feminist Theory and Antiracist Politics" (1989), Crenshaw mobilizes the legal example of diagraming an accident to point out the malleability of the intersection theory. Scholars have troubled intersectionality for being "gridlocked" or not accounting for the control of bodies through "affective capacities and tendencies," so I find it useful to return to Crenshaw's original example for what it offers this inquiry in terms of malleability and affective control.[53] Crenshaw notes that "it is not always easy to reconstruct an accident: Sometimes the skid marks and the injuries simply indicate that they occurred simultaneously, frustrating efforts to determine which driver caused the harm."[54] In this metaphor, the accident's causes may be multiple—both knowable and unknowable. Extending the metaphor for a moment: the accident could be caused by the drivers, the road, the pedestrians, or poor signage, any of which includes the possibility of affective control by a larger structural entity. Moreover, the accident metaphor relies on a sense of motility, since identities are not static, nor are they understood in this framework as acting equally at the same time. Indeed, the idea of the intersection requires that one encounter it, approach it, or deliberately traverse it—eking out the space for intersectionality to think through identities as in flux and in processes of becoming as well as being spatially and temporally contingent.

Though I make use of the fold and I mention the processes of becoming, I am clear that I do not wish to take up another Deleuzian framework that has been proposed to accompany intersectionality: the assemblage. Jasbir Puar proposed that intersectionality be complemented by Deleuze and Guattari's assemblage.[55] Her rationale is that the "geopolitics of reception" does not deploy intersectionality to its original end.[56] I share Puar's concern that intersectionality has been misused to recenter whiteness and does not move smoothly across transnational borders, a concern voiced by Nirmala Erevelles, Julia Livingstone, and Clare Barker, as noted above. Yet, it is troubling that a theory crafted by and for Black women would be used to erase them again.[57] Intersectionality is an epistemological intervention: it reorients how and from whom we understand the Enlightenment project. Redirecting that orientation back to Deleuze and Guattari (especially given that Hortense Spillers's work anticipates and expands Deleuze's ideas about the fold) reasserts the import of white European epistemologies over and against those of Black women and validates continental European intellectual traditions as standard. Taking a cue from Brittney Cooper's project in *Beyond Respectability: The Intellectual Thought of Race Women* (2017), I understand Black women's intellectual projects as schools of thought that from the nineteenth century onward sought to prioritize the specificity of Black women's embodied theorizing.[58] Since intersectionality arises out of that intellectual space, evacuating Black women from it prioritizes an ideology that abets their erasure. To foist assemblage onto intersectionality also reduces Black women's embodied theorizing and becomes merely another vehicle for the enactment of privilege since it shifts the conversation away from them and their ideas about world-making.[59] It is in the nature of privilege to find ever more places to hide. Accounting for this, I find that despite the fact that the assemblage and the fold share a similar emphasis on process, the assemblage (as a concept for discussing identity) brings with it a set of ideas that does not suit my inquiry.

What I am also unwilling to take with the theory of assemblage is the freighted territory of the cyborg: the feminist materialist theory of becoming developed by Donna Haraway that combines human, animal, and machine as a radical political enterprise that ushers in the future both theoretically and practically. I have found it useful as a thought exercise that complicates the relationship of the body to itself and to others and deals with our very real reliance on machines and kinship with animals. Since the cyborg opens up the conversation about futurity—which usually elides madness and Blackness—it also becomes a useful space to consider who we are becoming.[60] Certainly, to think through our kinship with machines is apropos for discussions of disability given the medicalization of certain bodies, and remains so given my emphasis on speculative fiction. But the cyborg is an incomplete, politically fraught, and ethically suspicious answer to a series of questions about raced and disabled futurity. Material reality must reckon with what others have pointed out are the lived experiences of the Black and disabled body, what amount to (in this project, at least) the gaps and folds within Black speculative fiction. Read in alignment with Tobin Siebers's theory of complex embodiment and Alison Kafer's questioning of spatial, cultural, and temporal logics, the emphasis on the cyborg and the desire to supersede the body has an antagonistic relationship with concerns at the heart of disability studies: pain, fiscal access, and the validity of embodied experience, to name a few.[61] What happens when one does not desire cyborgian intervention as cure? What of those for whom material cyborgian realities are more painful than useful or pleasurable? As much as cyborgian futures promise a radical set of possibilities for considering disability, we ought to be wary of them because they are also reliant on a set of middle-class (or rich) realities.

I have elsewhere pointed out the way the cyborg's promise of radical potential hinges on an original white Western subject.[62] Leaning on Donna Haraway's original definition, João Costa Vargas and Joy A. James understand the Black cyborg as a postbellum construction that requires Black degradation: "A Black cyborg: a modified, improved human whose increased ethical, spiritual, and physical capabilities generate unusual strength, omniscience, and boundless love."[63] They invoke Haraway's understanding of the cyborg as both real and fictive to pinpoint how the Black cyborg relies on a set of interracial dynamics that extend from a history steeped in anti-Blackness. The Black cyborg is required to participate in its own self-abnegation since it is built on top of the foundations of American democratic and imperial projects reliant on phobic understandings of Blackness. The Black cyborg, then, in Vargas and James's formulation, echoes that of the disabled cyborg: neither can escape the desire for normalcy that erases Blackness and madness both. Alison Kafer reads in the gaps of Haraway's work and its intellectual genealogy to reinsert the oft-overlooked contributions of women of color—among them Octavia E. Butler and Chela Sandoval—to the definition of the cyborg. She pinpoints that the cyborg as transgressive figure has limited potential precisely because of how it has been developed and mobilized in ways that erase women of color and reify the virgule between disabled and able-bodied. Though the cyborg asks for blasphemous interpretation—a promise and proposition Kafer, Vargas, and James readily champion—as part of its political transgression, I question how much the cyborg can map a future of any kind when it relies on a past and path of erasure. What the cyborg ushers in—that I'd prefer to leave aside for this discussion—is an assemblage yoked to anti-Blackness and ableism, a method of becoming that requires theoretical overcoming since the theories rely on but refuse disabled and Black embodiment.

The sections that follow function as a conversation about madness and Blackness, each one questioning and returning to the ones before to uncover, recover, discover the relationships between these two concepts. They are not, as mentioned in the preface, meant to form a narrative arc. My intention in bringing madness and Blackness together theoretically is not to create a linear narrative about the constellation of relationships that comprise the two. Instead, I wish to open up several interrelated conversations that intertwine, agree, and, perhaps, rebuke each other. Each section begins with a discussion of the critical literature as an inroad to raising questions that scholars have overlooked or elided. I segue into the fictive texts, not as illustrative examples of the critical conversations but rather as interventions. The artists-theorists in this study press us to pause in the breaks of the critical literature and undergo another process of intussusception. Their work revamps how we might think about the questions we raise regarding Blackness and madness and the relationships between the two.

The first conversation, "Making Black Madness," examines the somewhat canonical idea that race and disability mutually constitute each other. Tracing this idea through its genesis in disability studies, I find that this idea only leaves room for recuperative historical or emancipatory projects. Octavia E. Butler's *Fledgling* (2005) intervenes in its depiction of Black madness, theorizing about the way intimate relationships disrupt the impulses that undergird mutual constitution. Ultimately, Butler interrogates whether the concept of mutual constitution is a useful reading strategy. The second discussion, "A Mad Black Thang," parses mental illness and cognitive ability to think about what happens when madness exists in the context of Blackness. I argue for the concept of mad Blackness, since it invalidates Western dependence on ocularity and linear progression by shifting conceptions about or amplifying the reaches of Blackness and madness. As a sonic novel, Nalo Hopkinson's *Midnight Robber* (2000) meditates on the potentials of silence and putative mad speech. Hopkinson's work allows for mad Blackness to transform how we conceptualize madness within intraracial spaces.

Following a politics of curiosity, in the third conversation, "Abandoning the Human?," I ask what it might mean to unmake Black madness. That is, how might we disengage with the ideas that undergird these concepts? Tananarive Due's conception of the nonhuman in her *African Immortals* series (1997–2011) shifts the discursive terrain by questioning what it means to desire Blackness, how and why (cognitive) ability continues to have ideological weight, and what interpretive strategies exist that privilege mad Black epistemologies. Her series functions as a heuristic that allows us to test how and why Blackness and madness acquire critical purchase in a world designed for their erasure. Due's work also presses critics to articulate when and why we might abandon the concept of the human—residues of the Enlightenment project—in favor of Blackness and madness. In the final section, "Not Making Meaning, Not Making Since (The End of Time)," I question the ideological conceit at the heart of both disability studies and Black studies, when viewed from the standpoint of a linear progressive narrative—that Blackness and madness must mean something. Here I commit an act of literary theorist blasphemy by trying to sort through which conditions would make it possible for Black madness to lose meaning but not value. Understanding Mat Johnson's irreverent Black mad characters as a starting point for such musings, I conjecture about what happens to the Black mad and the mad Black at the end of time. As mentioned earlier, I turn to the way Johnson describes and engages the novel specifically because the genre presumes the validity of linear progressive narratives. Johnson's work not only questions the possibilities within the novel but also permits *Black Madness :: Mad Blackness* to pan outward beyond Black speculative fiction to think about what Black novels do writ large. Caveat: this book does not have a conclusion. As I explain in more detail in the preface and in the final section, reading and theorizing mad Blackness and Black madness demands an elliptical openness that refuses linearity and progression toward traditional conclusions. Rather than artificially foist one upon this discussion, I've chosen to leave it somewhat open. This is a mad Black book, after all.

I mobilize the malleability of intersectionality and the de facto validity of embodied, lived experience for the purposes of this conversation. Rather than recenter the conversation on whiteness as a guiding paradigm, I choose to examine the places where normativity breaks: the accident in the middle of the intersection, as it were. My readings focus on the gaps, mistakes, folds, and breaks. I assess the damage, and provide a lens for reading Blackness and madness together. To my mind, the mad Black/Black mad subject is not simply standing at an intersection but also actively changing it. In what follows, I seek to figure out how.

:: CONVERSATION I

MAKING BLACK MADNESS

request :: *familiar pause*
innocence :: backpedal
Dear Scar Tissue,
I want my softness to be safe.

—KHADIJAH QUEEN,
"Black Peculiar :: Energy Complex,"
Black Peculiar

"As it stands, Disability Studies has a tenuous relationship with race and ethnicity: while the field readily acknowledges its debt to and inspiration by inquiries such as Black Studies, its efforts at addressing intersections between ability, race, and ethnicity are, at best, wanting," the late Christopher M. Bell intones.[1] His book chapter, "Introducing White Disability Studies: A Modest Proposal," widely considered the inaugural moment in Black disability studies, sardonically does not—in true Swiftian fashion—call for an overhaul of methodology, analysis, and representation.[2] Bell provokes scholars to seek and find the places where race and disability intersect, write about those spaces, and promote structural change to the field. He also urges affective shifts in the way scholars embrace each other and others within the field. Given the venue of his book chapter, *The Disability Studies Reader* (second edition), Bell's work speaks to a particular audience invested in disability studies already. In 2011, the introduction to his posthumously released edited collection, *Blackness and Disability: Critical Examinations and Cultural*

Interventions, pans outward, staging "an intervention into the structuralist body politics underpinning African American studies and the whiteness at the heart of Disability Studies."[3] These two inaugural moments press for more granularity in the way of analysis that did little more than say race was like disability and vice versa. (Unfortunately, those "like race" analogies still crop up.) Instead, Bell advocates a set of projects that rereads figures— historical, literary, and cultural—who have been overlooked for their contributions to Black notions of disability or disabled notions of Blackness. Within the volume, scholars focused on specifically Black cultural locations of disability engaged with ableist attitudes, and foregrounded how Blackness alongside disability heralded radicality of a certain kind.

Seemingly in answer to Bell's work, scholars developed a reading strategy that clarifies how race and disability operate: mutual constitution. Specifically, mutual constitution impresses upon readers how these two discourses operate as interrelated and simultaneously present. This reading strategy performs several useful functions within the scholarship. In the interest of carving space to examine our critical conversations and open them up with the work of artists-theorists, I turn to several key moments in our use of mutual constitution to think through when it works and when it does not. This critical reading strategy becomes useful when understanding how disability has been used as a discursive tool. For example, racial and gendered groups have tended to justify their cases for civil rights in opposition to individuals with disabilities. The rhetorical invocation of disability here only functions to undergird the validity of another people groups' personhood (at the expense of the personhood of the disabled).[4] Disability, in this case, does not quite exist as a material reality but rather as a hauntological presence that helps create race and gender, sometimes as superlative. In thinking of race and disability as material, one must consider that contexts of oppression and war create disability, often with detrimental effects on those already disenfranchised by institutional racism.[5] In this case, disability shores up the physical evidence of institutionalized racism and systemic injustice, helping to define race as a matter of life and death.

In addition to highlighting the discursive and material effects of race and disability in tandem, such mutuality also serves an argumentative function. Since it is a critical reading practice, it also shapes how critics write about the two subjects. This project, in its interest in opening up the critical literature to itself, invests in discussing this as a writing and reading strategy for how it roadmaps intellectual possibility (and, as the metaphor goes, closes off certain avenues). Within Ellen Samuels's monograph *Fantasies of Identification: Disability, Gender, Race* (2014), she pinpoints that "the mutual entangled and constitutive dynamic of disability, gender, and race in modern fantasies of identification determines the shape and trajectory of [her] book" and, in articulating her main argument, states that "if, at times, one of these embodied social identities comes to the foreground, such that parts of the book address disability or race or gender more centrally, the overarching argument remains structured around the inseparability of their meanings."[6] An incredibly useful proposition. Samuels's caveat guarantees that readers do not miss the way that all discussions heavily rely on each other. Historically speaking, the creating of disability, race, and gender occurs at the same time. The strands of what would become modern medicine worked to differentiate bodies from each other, specifically normal bodies from abnormal ones, where abnormal was constituted in gendered, raced, and abled terms. These fantasies of identification found their justification in what Samuels terms "biocertification,"[7] a process that further links the construction of abnormality (and with it the construction of Blackness and disability) to objective science, aspiring to some semblance of truth. What becomes clear is not just that one cannot read race without disability nor disability without race, but that their entanglement requires a robust critical armature that grapples with them both.

When I trace the use of mutual constitution, two critical reading practices emerge: first, recuperation projects that seek to historicize, and, second, retrieval projects that read against ableism to find agency. In this way, mutual constitution performs as scholarly shorthand for "It's complicated." Intussuscepted (that is, enfolded) in these readings are several challenges to the practices themselves: specifically, scholarship is stagnated between recuperation and resistance. What of the projects that are neither? Is there a space between these or next to them, narratologically speaking? How can we read the moments when race and disability have a wider range of relationships? In what follows, I read the spaces where the critical material breaks open the possibilities for new readings of Blackness and disability in tandem. Though much of this material analyzes Blackness and disability broadly, I find that the distillate reveals the critical material to itself, suggesting that madness, Black madness in particular, troubles the impulses of retrieval and radicality. First, Blackness and madness encounter the problem of existing on the same temporal plane, particularly when whiteness is a factor. The Black mad subject gets evacuated from history while the white able subject or white disabled subject dictates the terms of history's narration. Second, Black mad subjects cannot always serve as the prompts for others' freedom from ableism. It is possible for Black individuals, institutions, and cultural spaces to be ableist. Moreover, when Black spaces function as examples of freedom for others, they do not exist on their own terms, a logical concern that lands us back in the terrain where whiteness instrumentalizes Blackness for its own ends. Later in this conversation, I turn to Octavia E. Butler's *Fledgling* (2005) and her archive for how she theorizes Blackness and madness.[8] Butler's texts and her archive offer alternative analytic strategies to the problems posed by mutual constitution in its current form.[9]

Recuperating, Historicizing

Mutual constitution attends to the fiction of fixity often ascribed to race and disability writ large. Reading race and disability in this way yokes the discourses to each other, since they typically cannot be pinned down elsewhere. When Ellen Samuels traces the way this mutual constitution functioned within the nineteenth century, she finds that the discourses that created and sustained ideas about race and ability were not only created at the same time but also reliant on each other for validity. These national fantasies were created by physicians who scrupulously searched the body for clues about its difference.[10] Both the physically or mentally abnormal body and the racially abnormal body were understood as close cousins, demonstrating in their difference the validity and supremacy of the white able body by contrast. Samuels writes, "At the core of the fantasy of identification lies the assumption that embodied social identities such as race, gender, and disability are fixed, legible, and categorizable. This assumption, by now deeply naturalized in our social and ontological structures, in fact required elaborate construction and ongoing policing through the nineteenth century and early twentieth."[11] The very mutability of these social categories makes necessary the fiction of their fixity and the necessity of their policing by parties for whom that mutability causes concern. Mutual constitution offers a conceptual corrective, given the discursive history, and allows for an analysis to take shape around that history and the cultural context of its object(s) of inquiry.

Ensuring that this corrective attends to history authorizes critics to acknowledge the plasticity of Blackness and madness in tandem. Consider that the United States census of 1840 was the first to provide statistics about mental illness. The faulty statistics counted a higher incidence of madness among Blacks in the North at numbers that far exceeded the amount of Black people full stop. This pseudoscientific evidence not only arrogated madness to Blackness generally but also provided putative proof that Blacks were unfit for freedom, claiming that free Blacks were eleven times more likely to have mental illness than the enslaved or white populations.[12] The postbellum environment does not undergo a dramatic shift in this regard; the definitions of Blackness available hinge on definitions of sanity. Kim Nielsen's *A Disability History of the United States* (2012) traces the early conception of citizenship as tied not only to enslavement but to mental illness as well.[13] This connection and its mutability continue into the mid-twentieth century when wider public scrutiny of mental health institutions (and some scandal), advocacy from the family of president John F. Kennedy, and civil rights discourse made it possible to imagine integrating mentally ill and cognitively disabled people into public spaces.[14] This integration effort occurs simultaneous to that which occurred for Black people, linking the two populations in the public sphere. This history pertains mostly to those categorized as mentally ill or cognitively disabled. Though the definition of madness for this text is more expansive than that (given the healthy skepticism of psy-disciplines based on this history), sketching the relationships between the two discourses and social identities over time permits a closer look at how Blackness and madness rely on each other for concretization. Such an analysis also reveals how tenuous they are. This history makes clear that within the United States's cultural zeitgeist, there is no Blackness without madness, nor madness without Blackness. Yet, the discourses' fragility suggests that the two have been forced together out of political convenience and presumed abjection.

Notwithstanding the utility of mutual constitution as a historicizing tool, it cannot—as a methodology—fully account for how race and disability interact on a body or between bodies. To be mutually constituted implies a reciprocity of creation. I put pressure on reciprocity because mutual implies simultaneity while occupying the temporal plane. I put pressure on creation because constitution assumes that, where discourses or material conditions related to race and disability exist, they develop and are sustained completely and consistently. In other words, the phrase mutual constitution implies race and disability announce themselves at the same time and both exert pressure in constant fashion. Case in point: Michelle Jarman's work exposes this fold. In her hermeneutic reading of lynch mobs and eugenic discourse, she writes that the two discourses are "not equal or competing" but rather "dynamic social and discursive processes that inform each other."[15] What her rhetorical sleight of hand allows is the possibility that one discourse will occupy more space than another or affect the material reality more than the other particularly within interracial encounter. Jarman pinpoints the hefty pull of eugenics discourse on the eventual castration of Benjy Compson (in Faulkner's *The Sound and the Fury*). Because the action of the novel takes place during the early twentieth century, she links this eugenics discourse to the pervasive nature and likely rationales for lynch mob murders. Though her link to lynch mobs undergirds her argument by positioning the two discourses as reliant on each other, her readings reveal that they do not affect material reality equally. For instance, Jarman's opening gambit points to a tragic illustration of when both ableist and racist discourses collide in the real life beating of Billy Ray Johnson, a Black cognitively disabled man, and its aftermath. Here, the full force of racist eugenics comes to bear on the availability of justice for Johnson. There is a slippage in the way these two discourses occupy space: news outlets, civil rights organizations, and law enforcement could not conceptualize Johnson as both Black and cognitively disabled (I say more about this invisibility in the second discussion). He was either one or the other in their imagination. The material consequence — suspended sentences and probation for his assailants instead of jail time — exacerbates the violence already inflicted. What Jarman's example reveals is that race and disability do vie for narrative space and, in this instance, determine material consequence based on which narrative is told and which is believed. Billy Ray Johnson's story ghosts that of Faulkner's Benjy because it undermines how we read the interlocking ideas about Blackness and madness within *Sound and the Fury*.

Here lies the critical lacuna we have yet to address. The historicization approach to discussions about race and disability presumes a linear progression of time, an unfolding that takes place at a pace to which we have become accustomed delineated by demarcations of second, minute, hour, day, month, and year. However, as calendars themselves often lay bare, few cultures think of time in the same way. Which New Year do you celebrate? Is your calendar lunar or solar? Time does not progress in the same fashion for everyone. It becomes useful to think of history in terms of the fold. Here, I yoke Spillers's concept of the flesh with Deleuze's understanding of the fold (a point of connection between ideas where one begets the other) to Fred Moten's conceptualization of being, living, writing, meaning "in the break" (where history and narrative converge — invaginate or intussuscept, to use his terms—as a requisite part of being intertwined). If we are to linger in the fold, in the break, then we must reckon with the way madness and Blackness force us to render history countermnemonically: attending to gaps, mistakes, deferrals, silences, glitches. It is in this break, cut, fold that the relationship between Blackness and madness becomes most clear. Here is the relationship between Blackness and disability writ large, a relationship sutured at times by its connections, but also turned in and turned out by missed connections, erasures, and gaps.[16]

Despite the fact that both disability and race as ideas emerged at the same moments in history, they do not necessarily occupy the same temporal plane when conjoined in quotidian interaction. In thinking of interracial encounter for instance, Sharon P. Holland reminds us of a "persistent problem in the Black/white encounter," specifically that we must question "what happens when someone who exists in time meets someone who only occupies space?"[17] As she delineates, Blackness appears as the antithesis of history, its excretion, whereas whiteness stands in for progression, being in time. Our sense of the two interacting in the same moment then is skewed by the fact that Blackness is not meant to be a part of history but rather its object. Black cultural production has consistently expanded upon this idea through its skepticism of linear progressive narratives that assume Western origins, choosing instead to position Africa (usually the continent, broadly conceptualized) as a futuristic space or elide Western notions of time and space.[18] Thinking through the Black mad subject, we must consider that this person is meant not only to occupy space but to be consistently removed from space in order to make room for the more recognizable subject: the white able body. It is this body that dictates the terms of history and narrative. In the case of Billy Ray Johnson, the criminal justice system determined that his assailants were allowed to move on with their lives regardless of the violence and damage done to his body. If we are to consider Bell's modest proposal, the Black mad subject is removed from time to make space for the white disabled body as well. In other words, the Black disabled subject exists only to shore up the value of others. So, when the Black/white encounter is divided along ability lines such that the disabled body is white and the able body is Black, what emerges is a dynamic of relationships that force Blackness and disability into the realm of unspeakability, troubling the idea that both are created and sustained at the same time.

The second critical impulse, retrieval projects that read against ableism to find agency, attempts to locate spaces of resistance where race and disability meet. Here again, I turn to the critical conversations to read where the distillate reveals the material to itself. An analysis of resistance surfaces as part of projects undertaking Bell's "representational detective work" that "uncovers the misrepresentations of Black, disabled bodies and the missed opportunities to think about how those bodies transform(ed) systems and culture."[19] As such, it offers a way to think through the cultural and political contours of structural ableism as intersected with structural racism. So far, this scholarship concludes that Black disabled bodies loosen the grip of ableism by resisting cultural norms of both disabled and Black communities: scholars explore this dynamic within Blackness and madness from a wide variety of critical angles, including Black women and depression (Anna Mollow), melancholia and poverty (Éva Tettenborn, Anne Cheng, Paul Gilroy), cognitive disability and civil rights redress (Stacie McCormick), rehabilitation and Black queerness (Robert McRuer), and popular music (Nicole Fleetwood, La Marr Jurelle Bruce, Moya Bailey, Anna Hinton). Usefully, this body of scholarship opens up the critical space left closed when we aver that discourses of Blackness and madness compete. Each points out that the workings of structural racism and ableism do not complement each other. In fact, the cultural logics that mandate Blackness as abject can depose those that maintain disability as such.

This strategy is not the only or primary way to read challenges to racism and ableism. The problem exists (*pace* Hortense Spillers) at the level of grammar. These projects tend to have one vector: they "transform(ed) systems and culture."[20] Note that transform operates as transitive where Black, disabled bodies perform the work of transformation rather than undergo the process of transformation. Yet Black, disabled bodies will not always behave as agents that transform or those who are transformed in equal measure or, as noted above, with a degree of reciprocity. Allowing for more than one vector between Black, disabled bodies and the systems in which they operate clarifies the following: it is inaccurate that the only critical relationship between Blackness and disability (specifically, madness) is one of liberation from ableism. At times, Blackness exacerbates the presence of ableism, or cultural norms facilitate ableism.[21] In accounting for these moments, I trouble the corollary of the logic above: namely, that whiteness withal the privilege embedded in it lacks the tools for its own liberation and must rely on Blackness to acquire its release. Here, Blackness becomes a reduced space where whiteness enacts its privilege by instrumentalizing Blackness. In this paradigm, Blackness for all its cultural complexity becomes another reactionary space that exists to indict whiteness, rather than a culture and system of thought all its own.[22] We must consider the spaces when mere exposure of oppression is not only not emancipatory but can also be detrimental, where demonstration and acknowledgement of one's various intersecting socially marginalized positions does not equal political agency. We must also consider what happens when Black cultural locations refuse whiteness as an interlocutor in favor of intraracial conversations. In short, when madness is "a Black thang" (with all that evokes in terms of exclusivity and ableist objectification).

I take up the question of intraracial context and conversation in the next discussion. For now, I turn to another foundational moment in the study of Blackness and disability to read in the breaks of the critical material. I continue the conversation about the critical impulse of mutual constitution that looks to retrieve agentive stories of Black disabled folks as instantiations of anti-ableist radicality. Rosemarie Garland Thomson's *Extraordinary Bodies* (1997) includes a chapter on physical disability in Ann Petry's *The Street*, Toni Morrison's oeuvre, and Audre Lorde's *Zami*. Though Thomson's discussion does not explicitly discuss mental disability, cognitive impairment, or crazy-as-insult, I find it instructive for this conversation. Madness shadows each of the texts under scrutiny since the characters deviate from intracultural norms by being Black women who seek class ascension despite the odds (Petry) and wider American cultural norms by participating in and identifying with communities labeled deviant (and crazy) by the DSM IV (Lorde). Of course, Morrison's characters are literally haunted by their actions and kinfolk, which always forces the question of whether Morrison's characters could be labeled crazy. It becomes useful to think about Morrison's, Petry's, and Lorde's work (especially as part of Garland Thomson's project) from the perspective of Octavia E. Butler: namely, that sanity is communally defined and anyone who deviates from agreed upon norms is treated as mad. The characters' desires for themselves (and the methods they use to achieve them) exceed the racialized and gendered boundaries drawn for them. Indeed, because they also have physical disabilities, their behavior trespasses the boundaries drawn based on ability as well. Madness cannot be cleaved from these conversations. Thomson's claims about the representation of physical disability as agentive and liberatory have implications for whether madness has similar representational possibilities.[23]

Thomson offers that the collective project of these Black women's writings provides an antidote to white racist depictions. These powerful bodies—extraordinary, in Thomson's lexicon—participate in a "collective project of cultural revision [that] challenges the African-American woman writer to produce a narrative of self that authenticates Black women's oppressive history yet offers a model for transcending that history's limitations."[24] Moreover, the primacy given to disabled women figures "reveals the shift in African-American literary representation from a modernist to a postmodernist mode, a change that parallels the ideological move of minority groups from assimilation to affirmation of cultural and ethnic differences."[25] While I partly agree that these representations "render oppression without reinscribing it,"[26] I hesitate to read in them the triumph that Thomson affirms. On the one hand, Thomson rightly points out that these characters do not completely represent physical deviance. On the other, they do not, as she says, "repudiate such cultural master narratives as normalcy, wholeness, and the feminine ideal."[27] I would attribute this aspect of their representation to the way that the social model of disability upon which Thomson relies does not fully account for the way madness shows up in these texts.[28] The social model privileges a particular kind of mental agility and cognitive processing to combat the stigma and material consequences that arise as a result of ableism. In turn, the model dismisses madness as a viable subject position, ensuring that those counted as such—either by communal consensus or psy-disciplines—remain excluded from conversations about disability because they cannot logically engage. For the characters in Thomson's study, this has the pernicious effect of erasing some of the master cultural narratives they work against: those that acknowledge their physical disability and link it to mental disability as a way to further disenfranchise and disempower them.

Thomson's work reads these figures (based on their representation of physical disabilities) as liberatory for the larger narrative and theoretical spaces of ethnic modernism. I hazard that these characters' relationship to disability suggests an investment in internalized ableism, particularly vis-à-vis sexuality. For example, Thomson reads Ann Petry's Mrs. Hedges, a tall, dark-skinned Black woman with avoirdupois who works as a madam, as one who refuses victimization. Important for this conversation is the way Mrs. Hedges is not only physically disfigured by burns but also read as exceeding the gendered and racialized boundaries the text's Black community (voiced through the protagonist) circumscribes for her. Her madness is not biomedically defined, but it carries psychosocial repercussions given how she is treated. Thomson bases her reading of Mrs. Hedges as liberatory on Hedges's sexualized gaze on the main character and her profession as a madam. Yet, there is no room for Hedges to acquiesce to or enjoy the sexualized attention she receives from the rich white man who controls the street. The novel makes it clear that part of Hedges's rejection of the man's sexual advances is financial. She cannot be in bed with him literally and economically. However, what the novel leaves open is that Hedges's rejection of him is also about her own denigrated view of her sexuality.[29] She is still limned as monstrous, grotesque, even if Hedges as a figure shifts the understanding of monstrosity. Inasmuch as Hedges's physical disability allows her to move from one position in the economy to another more powerful one, she must rely on a chosen life of celibacy and a masculinized, monstrous appearance to secure and maintain her new economic position. Her celibacy also shores up her power by keeping the madness of her disfigured, disabled, interracial sexuality in check. That is, though the disability is no longer in the background of the text, the cultural baggage of internalized ableism appears in the foreground replete with eschewing sexual desire and limiting the association with traditional forms of femininity. Even if Petry's project does—according to Thomson—pave the way for Black authors to shift from assimilation to affirmation and provide a challenge to the static representations of disabled figures in modernist texts, Mrs. Hedges's refusal to engage in her own sexuality complicates a reading of this figure as liberatory vis-à-vis physical disability and the charges of madness that accompany her character.

Reading Mrs. Hedges as agentive certainly poses challenges given the internalized ableism within Petry's text, especially since the novel focuses on intraracial encounter. First, physical disability only liberates Mrs. Hedges from the intraracial economy of the street by providing an avenue for power. Yet, within intraracial encounter, she remains circumscribed by the discourses of madness because community members consider her mad for transgressing boundaries of race and gender. Second, the interracial encounter does not allow for her agency within the critical literature. Thomson claims that Petry's text, as well as the others, counters the limited representations of disability within modernist texts. Implicitly, the logic of such a critical move—regardless of its truism—mandates that Blackness become the vehicle for (mostly white) others' liberation from ableism in their reading practice. In that way, it is the presence of Blackness that shores up white liberalism by not only providing a representation of Blackness but also a complex rendering of white-centered notions of disability.

Elsewhere, I have argued similarly—that we ought to attend to the way that Blackness and whiteness function in the interracial multiability encounter. In my article on television's *Monk*, I proposed that Blackness and madness cannot take up the same space within one interaction. I read the protagonist's unnamed obsessive-compulsive disorder as a disability that "misfits" with other (usually minor) characters' Blacknesses.[30] At times, one is used for comedic fodder or erased in favor of representing the other or eclipsed as a way to demonstrate white liberalism. My article describes the relationship between these two identities as mutually constituted, but it evinces some slippage when attempting to discern why the protagonist's disability erases the other characters' Blackness. Since Blackness and madness do not reside in the same body, the various drama-comedy scripts tergiversate about what difference among difference can mean, often mobilizing white liberalism to police disability and Blackness. Rereading my own work with an eye toward the breaks, I find that we not only lack a critical vocabulary for describing Blackness and madness simultaneously, but it is also assumed that one must take priority over the other. The end result is that in this interracial encounter—whether fictionalized, theorized, or criticized—either Blackness or madness must be erased. Important for this conversation is that the multiracial, multiability encounter shifts depending on the social position of the characters. Blackness cannot and should not be marshaled as the radical space for white liberalism to mount its critique of ableism or racism. When Blackness and madness exist in the same space, multiple ways of reading should become possible, some of which eschew the possibility of radicality and others that might usher it in.

The multiability interracial encounter also allows for Blackness and madness to be erased when improperly thought of as agentive. Because both discourses are often conceptualized as unspeakable or illegible, their presence can facilitate and consolidate the power that creates abject material conditions. Nirmala Erevelles makes this point most forcefully: "The analytic category of disability is useful in destabilizing static notions of identity, exploring intersectionality, and investigating embodiment, [yet] I argue that the effectiveness of much of feminist disability studies remains limited because of its overreliance on metaphor at the expense of materiality."[31] In other words, Blackness and disability have the potential to destabilize the rhetoric of normalcy that holds them as abject, but they are curtailed in doing so when mislabeled as agentive. In Erevelles's exploration of the lived conditions of war, she argues that when disability (both physical and mental) intersects with Black and brown bodies in the developing world or in disenfranchised communities within the developed world, their confluence indicts unchecked multinational corporate greed because it reveals the politicized nature of impairment. With this in mind, there can be no ableist or racist narrative available that prioritizes individualized achievement (read: overcoming) or bemoans bad luck (read: pity) because the root cause implicates specific governments, companies, the people who run them, and those who are complicit in them. In addition, Erevelles resists ascribing agency to the disabled people of color she discusses, perhaps because, in this version of David and Goliath, Goliath is winning. More to the point, the material conditions for celebration and agency require material resources not available to everyone, and mere knowledge of one's situation cannot be proxy for freedom from it, nor does awareness equal agency.

Fledgling and in Search of *Asylum*

So, the critical task before us is not to dismiss mutual constitution but rather to develop a more robust analytic that does not remain stagnated between recuperation and resistance. We must consider how recuperative projects assume a simultaneity and reciprocity of creation not always present within linear history and interracial encounter. We must be wary of projects that locate resistance on Black mad bodies solely in service of white bodies (regardless of ability status), avoiding the seduction of ascribing agency at the cost of ignoring material reality. The critical literature foments its analysis based on characters or people's relationships to structures and institutions; yet, within each lurks the possibility of analyzing another set of relationships, the interpersonal. Without parsing structural violence and history from intimacy, Octavia E. Butler's consideration of kinship and intimate relationships offers a space to consider the quotidian and erotic praxis that undergirds the relationships and analytical possibilities of Blackness and madness. A move to the quotidian and the erotic prioritizes the import of "the discretionary acts and, yes, racist [and ableist] practices that each of us make in everyday decisions such as choosing someone to sit beside on the subway, selecting a mate or a sperm donor, or developing a list of subjects for an academic study."[32] Not only should we rethink the "autonomy usually attached to erotic choices" but also how "racism [and ableism] orders some of the most intimate practices of everyday life."[33] Obviously, proximity and intimacy offer no curative function for racism and ableism and can, in point of fact, exacerbate the wounds they create. Yet, the contours of how we discuss intimacy reverberate beyond the individuals it includes, revealing a limited threshold for complex interpretation.[34] When we do not excuse the behavior of allies, friends, family, and sexual partners as representative of a culture, poor impact of good intention, or part of a learning curve, they offer another way to think through the constellation of relationships between Blackness and madness, circumventing the inclination toward limited readings of either resistance or recuperation.

Both frustrating and fascinating, Black speculative fiction writer and pioneer Octavia E. Butler renders intimate, personal relationships with an eye toward complexity and compromise.[35] Her characters' investment in each other does not necessarily equate to a divestment from the oppressive ideologies that buoy their power. Most important for this inquiry, Butler's work foregrounds the spaces of discomfort and erasure that accompany Black madness. As noted in the preface and introduction, I view Butler as a theorist working in the medium of fiction. I analyze her archive and her final published novel *Fledgling* (2005), interpreting the intimate relationships she depicts. Here, I invest in the "politics of the possible" regarding modes of interpretation that function as alternatives to mutual constitution.[36] Elsewhere I have discussed the enemy relationships in Butler's *Fledgling*, pinpointing that the protagonist's enemies "[mobilize] racist rhetoric subsequent to failed ableist rhetoric."[37] Their motives and their ideas are easily understood as a threat to the protagonist's life, a desire for her erasure, since their engagement with Blackness and disability relies on a denigration of both. This discomfort and erasure flows from the protagonist's lovers, friends, and family as well. Here, the discourses of madness and Blackness vie for importance, a competition of sorts in which neither can win, but where the decision to prioritize one over the other shifts the emotional and ideological terrain, particularly in the interracial, multiability encounter. Butler theorizes that Black madness creates a crisis of the self in which subjectivity and identity is destabilized and the conception of the future altered.

Butler conceptualized *Fledgling* as a coming-of-age and chase narrative that follows the structure of a crime procedural. In a letter to her editor she writes, "This one is essentially Shori's [the protagonist's] struggle to rebuild her life in spite of her lost family and memory—and, of course, she can only rebuild if she finds those who are hunting her and her love ones and stop them. In *Law and Order* fashion, she does this first through physical action—looking for answers, finding them, getting surprised, fighting to stay alive.... Then there's the trial—a less physically active part of the story, but one just as involved in its own conflict and drama."[38] The first third of the novel follows Shori as she awakes with amnesia, learns that she is a vampire (called Ina) from her father, Iosif, and finds human companions, including Wright, Celia, and Brooke (called symbionts, abbreviated as syms) to survive. During this time, she learns that what separates her from other Ina is genetic experimentation with human blood that grants her melanin and the capacity to remain awake during the day. The middle third of the novel depicts her adjustment to her new symbionts, including three same-gender loving relationships with syms Theodora, Celia, and Brooke, and her alliance with the male Ina family to whom she was/is betrothed (the Gordons). The final third delineates the trial, or Council of Judgment, which determines truth and consequences for those Ina who attempted to murder her, and successfully murdered her family (Silk family, Dahlman family). Butler's notebooks and journals reveal that she conceptualized several sequels to *Fledgling*. She completed five chapters of a novel tentatively called *Asylum* or *Flight*. In it, she introduces a new symbiont, a newfound archive from Shori's mothers, and the drama of being kidnapped by unmated male members of the Silk family. In the journal entries months before her death, Butler rethinks the story line of kidnapping and considers the story of a seduction, where Shori must build a family of symbionts and Ina sisters.[39]

Within *Fledgling*, several intimate relationships—the Gordon family, Daniel Gordon, Shori's symbionts—clarify how Black madness disrupts the ideological field: their behavior clarifies that the reading strategy of mutual constitution elides the competition between Blackness and madness for narrative space, the impossibility of linear progressive understandings of history and time, and the fiction of Black mad resistance as always agentive. As a family, the Gordons remain in thrall to their able-bodied and race privilege, such that it governs their interpretations of Shori. They "deploy an evaluative gaze that assesses Shori's 'fitness' based on their own criteria—shaped as it is by abled embodiment. The Gordons constitute fitness based on criteria that demonstrate their ignorance about the systemic effect whiteness and ability have had on their lives."[40] Since they do not distinguish between her amnesia as impairment and Ina cultural and traditional customs as fomenting disability, they exude a paternalism that becomes taxing for Shori to navigate. She must consistently remind them that her impairment has practical implications to which their cultural structures (such as the Council of Judgment or mating rituals) must adapt.[41] She reminds them, "My memory goes back a few weeks and no further," and the narration explicates her emotional response, "And because I was annoyed. I let my tone of voice say, *You should all realize this. I've explained it before.*"[42] Further, they neglect to think of her Blackness as more than just the genetic engineering experimentation that allows her to be awake during the day. They consider her melanin useful as part of her physiology but do not think through the implications of how it creates her outsider status. The Gordons rank her identities: her Blackness as more beneficial, her amnesia as more pitiable, her Blackness as less important, her amnesia as less desirable. Their logic views the two identities as competitive in their narration of events: only one category requires their attention at any given time. Their priorities reveal how one identity, disability, is a problem for them that they can articulate. Her other identity, Blackness, is a problem to be sure, but one about which they cannot answer a word.[43] Further, it stresses that their deliberate problematizing of one identity parses Blackness and madness for their own comfort. When Butler portrays Shori as frustrated in addition to misunderstood, she debunks the idea that all one must do is fuse the identities together. In other words, it is not necessarily a problem that the Gordons must strategize about Shori's disability (especially since doing so will help save her life), but rather that they seek to strategize without fully understanding the disability itself (and how it is shaped by Blackness) and without her input.

In this instance, Black madness cannot be agentive or radical or resistant all by itself. Shori's mere presence cannot bear the weight of reorienting the narrative all on its own, nor can her behavior automatically shift the ideologies that govern her circumstances or change the people who helped create and sustain them (which, by default, includes the Gordon family). Instead, Butler's work suggests that allies themselves must reconcile the competing tension between their own privileged positions and their desires for inclusivity. Though Shori can marshal her embodied knowledge to instruct others, she has limited success. The Gordons' gaze functions similarly to that of Shori's enemies. Their intimate interaction highlights that the difference between the two—that is, good intention—requires more labor on Shori's part (which by itself curtails agency). She cannot dismiss the Gordons because they are not antagonists; instead, she must reframe the conversation to emphasize her position as potential daughter-in-law in need of assistance. When Shori reminds them, "So far [her] problem is ignorance, not dishonesty,"[44] she splices impairment from disability and suggests listening as an integral facet of engagement. Yet her interactions with the older Gordons remain taxing and frustrating because their good intentions do not match the impact of their behavior. Their remarks—she is "somewhat arrogant" or she must "seem more Ina than [the antagonists]," or she is "both very attractive and very frightening"[45]—belie their weddedness to ableism, even as they attempt to help her navigate institutionalized barriers. It is up to them to shift their thinking, and it is not clear that ever occurs by the end of *Fledgling*.

In Butler's drafts of *Fledgling*, she toys with the way Shori's Black madness structures her interactions with the Gordons and the text writ large. Each instantiation of the novel evinces Butler's commitment to depicting Blackness and madness as destabilizing forces, which heighten and problematize privilege because they shift the contours of the multiability, interracial encounter. The two discourses work together and, in that sense, remain coextensive, but they also function at cross-purposes. For instance, Shori speculates that the Gordons test her when they allow her to question the human agents responsible for the arson that killed her family. In Butler's drafts, she experiments with how to split the questioning between Shori and the Gordons, and, in the final version, Butler settles on Shori's silence. In the published version of *Fledgling*, Shori is only present to reassure the human agent and persuade him to tell the truth.[46] The effect of these changes—displacing the Gordons as the primary interrogators—suggests that the difference is not merely about the space given to the Gordons but rather how Blackness and madness operate. In one draft, Shori interrogates the human agent. Here, her Blackness functions as a discomfiting presence for the human, a reminder and remainder of her difference that forces him to reveal the identity of the Ina agents. Making her the interrogator does not disappear her madness, but it does emphasize a soundness of mind that does not appear to be consonant with her understanding of being Ina, undermining her general authority over her amnesiac experience. In another draft, the Gordons serve as the primary interrogators. Here, her Blackness performs a similar discomfiting function. Her amnesia bolsters her authority over her own experience, even as it forms the basis for her being surveyed by the Gordons. Her madness, invisibilized though it may be, structures the interaction since the Gordons' familiarity with other Ina allows them to ask leading questions of the human agent. By virtue of her amnesia, this is not an interrogation skill she can use. As a result, her silence in the face of her amnesia lingers as an answer to the Gordons' skepticism about her, creating two interrogations. In these drafts, splitting the questions between Shori and the Gordons reorganizes how and why information about the attacks is given, clarifying that Shori's Blackness and madness work on the interaction differently than the Gordons' whiteness and presumed sanity. In the final version of *Fledgling*, since she is largely silent, Shori's Black madness functions as a sustained pressure for the interrogation, emphasizing the Gordons' privilege in relation to her. Whereas her Blackness shores up her utility during the questioning, her madness strips away her authority and autonomy because the Gordons take over the interrogation of the human agent and, without saying a word about her amnesia, create an interrogation of her. Though her race is recognized in both the draft and the final copy as a boon to helping them catch and coerce the human agents, the difference in interrogation technique allows for her madness to reveal the Gordons' relationship to privilege.

Recall that thinking about Blackness and madness as mutually constituted leads us toward reading the two identities as an avenue toward agency when they are located on the same body. I objected to this line of thought because it requires that Blackness operate as a stepping stone for imagining agency only available under certain material conditions and assumes that mere knowledge of one's condition suffices as emancipatory. Butler's novel and archive theorizes about this in contemplating the interplay of desire and madness. Butler writes several drafts of an interaction between Shori and Daniel Gordon where Daniel, lost in his own desire for Shori, invites her to bite him.[47] In each draft, the invitation remains unspoken at first, functioning only as a matter of scent. He allows her to crawl all over him while they smell each other. The olfactory plays a large part in Ina attraction to either possible symbionts or other Ina. So, Daniel's invitation to smell—especially since he has to keep himself from acting on sexual arousal caused by her scent—is dangerously coercive. It suggests sexual agency for Shori, but in fact it jeopardizes her life. Butler writes what appears in the final version: Daniel's admission that he had hoped Shori's memory was impaired enough to let her bite him. He says, "I half-hoped you would [bite], that maybe with your memory gone, you would simply give in to my scent, my nearness. If you had, well . . . If you had, no one could prevent our union. No one would even try."[48] What keeps her from such an action is her understanding that it might threaten her good standing at the Council of Judgment. In these scenes, Daniel remains silent at first and, later, forthcoming about his desires/intentions. His invitation is a test, one Shori must pass to prove her Ina-ness to other council members, a perception of her identity dependent on both her race and her impairment. This is not merely about Daniel's desire but rather how his desire manifests as a form of ability that takes advantage of Shori's impairment and bears repercussions for the perception of her identity.

Operating along the axis of desire, Daniel's craving of Shori microaggresses her by circumscribing her within parameters that facilitate her erasure. Microaggressions as a series of environmental, verbal, and nonverbal slights often fall into the category of unintended discrimination and often occur in intimate and/or interpersonal spaces. At times, this discrimination also comes from an affective space of benevolence, where one intends to be nice but instead reveals one's own biases, ignorance, and desires. To read a microaggression, to understand it, is to analyze the break in the everyday since those moments prove revelatory about the microaggressor. Daniel intends to demonstrate desire and create intimacy, become Shori's Ina lover, and concretize what he views as the eventual mating between their families. However, Shori is not old enough in Ina society or physiologically mature enough to mate, and her impairment renders her ignorant of social customs regarding interaction between Ina males and females. In addition, Daniel has made a decision about his desire to mate with Shori, whereas Shori's ability to make such a decision must be—by virtue of her circumstances— delayed. Note the issue of time. Despite her enjoyment of Daniel's scent, Shori does not control the marketplace of desire, making murky the possibility of consent. Daniel's solicitation encourages her to break the rules and flirts with disaster given that they are on the cusp of a Council of Judgment meant to decide her fate.

It is crucial to note that within Butler's created worlds, biological imperatives are sacrosanct. In fact, she must remind both her editors that Daniel occupies a biologically subordinate role to Shori.[49] She writes to one editor, "I've done a little work on pages 143 through 144 as well as Chapter 21 to make it clear that Daniel is not dominant to Shori, that he is actually taking quite a risk when he offers himself to her, that chemically, the Ina are a matriarchy."[50] Despite his biologically subordinate role, Daniel's mental ability still affords him some power. In fact, it is Daniel's biological role that makes his coercion possible. He cannot compel Shori to bite him because of his masculinity. Instead, it is his intersected identity—as white, male, and able—that creates the parameters for him to perform such a microaggression.

Shori lacks the knowledge regarding social custom, which indicates why her sexual agency is a fiction. Whereas her madness opens up the space for her to name her sexual desire, when combined with her Black femaleness and the itinerant narratives associated with it (i.e., Jezebel), Shori's racialized and gendered madness actually strips her of sexual agency. Desire for Black madness foregrounds the idea that Blackness and madness exist on the spatial plane and whiteness, the temporal one: in other words, Shori's Black disabled body must be marshaled to constitute Daniel as a desiring subject. His lust not only takes him over but also obfuscates Shori in the process. Despite the first-person narration, Shori becomes subordinated to Daniel's initial desire. This not only occurs in the initial encounter but also gets used as leverage against Shori in the Council of Judgment when her main antagonist attempts to mobilize Daniel's desire as evidence against Shori. Black madness becomes the excretion of time, forced to occupy space while (white) others' desires (even if driven mad by said desire) occupy time. In temporal terms, Daniel's desire represents progression away from his family and into a future family with Shori (regardless of its feasibility), and the antagonists' rhetoric actively marks Shori as a moment of regression. Either way, she does not occupy temporal space as a being in time but instead functions as an object of time or a wrench in the machine, disrupting the progression of Daniel's family and, according to her antagonists, the progression of the Ina species.[51]

One of the fundamental relationships within the world of *Fledgling*, Ina-symbiont, is not only crucial for survival but also dictates the terms under which Black madness can be celebratory. Ina-symbiont relationships are symbiotic: Ina need their symbionts for companionship (constant touch, reassurance, conversation, sex) and food (blood). Symbionts become addicted to the venom of their Ina and grow to be dependent financially, psychologically, and chemically. Though the *Fledgling* novel only describes humans as symbionts, Butler's notes clarify that Ina are symbionts as well.[52] Butler had a long-standing fascination with symbiosis, not solely for what it offered in terms of conflict for a novel but also because she understood all life to be intimately connected.[53] When the Ina-symbiont relationship is mutual (as opposed to controlled entirely by an Ina's command), their interpersonal dynamics reveal how ideology becomes manifest in intimate relationships. Shori struggles in her relationships with her symbionts because she is re-learning how to be Ina, and they struggle with her because she does not seek to command or control their thoughts. Butler's depiction of their relationships refuses radical celebration of Shori's disability and also deliberately avoids positioning her as abject. Butler's text balances the refusal of degradation with others' attempt to interpellate her in those terms.

For example, Shori meets her primary symbiont (her first), Wright, a young white man, in the first third of the novel. He guesses that she is a vampire, pegs her as an amnesiac, and tells her that she is Black. Wright's reaction to Shori positions him as the first one to structure a relationship between Blackness and madness, between himself and Shori as a Black mad subject. He attempts to treat her as a wayward hitchhiking child and intends on taking her to the hospital until she bites him. After that, because of the intoxicating nature of her venom, they begin a sexual relationship. The fact that she looks eleven years old (and at this point readers have no idea that she is actually fifty-three) makes this an ostensibly pedophilic relationship. Pedophilia then becomes the primary way that Wright works through her Blackness and her madness. The intervening discourse for him is one of attraction and love, about which he is ashamed. Later, his resentment comes to the fore when Iosif (her father) explains to him that he may not have a choice as to whether he can leave her.[54] His attraction to her and his repulsion and resentment thereof compels him to become at times paternalistic caretaker. He teaches her about human rules, and helps structure the public face of her relationships with other symbionts (notably when he tells Shori and a Black symbiont Celia that they can pass as family). He struggles continuously with his subordinate relationship to Shori: he aggresses another (Black) male symbiont (Joel), complains to another (white) female symbiont (Brook), and resents his psychological addiction/need of Shori. In drafts of the sequel, another Ina tells Shori that Wright's behavior—trying to see how long he can stay away from Shori before he needs her venom—is his attempt to test her and is a period of adjustment that he must go through quickly. In another scene from that unpublished work, Wright quips, "What is it about you little bitty Black women? All you know how to do is give orders."[55] Ostensibly, his comment is about Celia, but it bears implications for Shori as well.

Butler crafts Wright as a character who cannot reconcile Shori's Black madness and his dependence. Their pedophilic sexual relationship becomes the avenue he uses to seek some degree of mastery and comfort. Yet, because her venom is seductive and their relationship mutualist, Wright's efforts foreground that Shori's Black madness only exacerbates the destructive potential of Wright's desire to adhere to white patriarchy. Whereas their pedophilic relationship ostensibly allows Wright the space to negotiate his power, the depth of his dependence plus the height of her power along with the inclusion of other symbionts foreclose his ability to navigate either her Blackness as authoritative figure or help treat her amnesia as able-bodied/ minded protector. When he first finds himself unable to cope, he responds with sexual violence. After meeting Iosif and his symbionts, Wright comes to terms with his loss of control and that given Ina custom, pedophilia is no longer the governing modality for understanding his interaction with Shori. He responds first with silent treatment, stonewalling, then with anger. Shori describes, "He rolled onto me, pushing my legs apart, pushing them out of his way, then thrust hard into me."[56] She responds with her bite, deeper than she intended, but matching his hard thrusts. Yet, if readers were to construe this as merely rough sex, their conversation troubles that interpretation. He asks whether he hurt her and she asks whether he wanted to. He responds in the affirmative.[57] The nature of consent isn't clear, but the violence intended is. Both her amnesia and her Blackness were navigable as illicit but not as consensual or acceptable. Wright has to possess Shori by force, subdue and control her somehow, if he is to consent to their relationship.

Consider the commonplace narratives about pedophilia as a sexualized madness (putting it mildly). To be clear, my reading here does not endorse these narratives but rather understands them as part of a cultural discourse that allows for madness to surface as an analytic. I keep with the definition of madness that maintains a tension between biomedical definitions (e.g., pedophilia as illness) and the psychosocial experience and usage (e.g., pedophilia as sexually deviant and criminal). Thinking of pedophilia in these terms acknowledges how Butler draws on these common discourses to theorize about how they are intertwined. This scene shifts the multiability interracial encounter in that the sexual violence between Wright and Shori dovetails with a familiar narrative about Black degradation and white madness: namely, that the latter is present only in the context of the former.[58] On the one hand, this narrative is dangerous because it dismisses the quotidian nature of racism and its structural quality. On the other, it forms the basis of a narrative facilitated by liberalism. By virtue of their incomprehensibility and socially unacceptable nature, morally reprehensible behaviors (lynching, hate crimes, sexualized violence, ableist violence, etc.) associated with oppressive ideology must be accompanied by madness. In these instances, madness becomes shorthand for explaining away or excusing unethical or outlandish behavior. Wright's desire to subjugate Shori, to violate her, participates in this familiar narrative. He can only understand the madness of his pedophilia in the context of her abjection. Yet, her amnesia, her madness, disrupts the denouement of this narrative. She matches him with her bite, not knowing or understanding his need for violence, thereby thwarting the possibility of her degradation and allowing for her own pleasure. It is her amnesia that cuts across Wright's own perception of his sexualized and racialized madness.

In thinking of Butler as a theorist, we cannot lose sight of the fact that "the use of Black women's language and cultural experience in books *by* Black women *about* Black women results in a miraculously rich coalescing of form and content and also takes their writing far beyond the confines of white/male literary structures."[59] That is, the intimacy of the novel, a pedagogical "monstrous intimacy" to use Christina Sharpe's language,[60] shifts as a result of privileging Black madness. Butler's aesthetic "[courts] the upheaval of traditional narratives by allowing disability to pervade the text," and, as a result, her work "unsettles ableist notions of form by highlighting with disability the contrapuntal relationship between the ableist world and the text."[61] *Fledgling*, within its structure, accounts for Shori's differences as a Black, female, amnesiac vampire. Specifically, the novel does not allow for the linear progressive understanding of time and narration but rather endorses the multiplicity courted by folds and gaps. In Butler's notes, this meditation takes the form of ellipses in the writing. In her drafts, Butler includes ellipses not as placeholders but as parts of the dialogue and narration. The gaps there do the work of creating silence and pausing within the narrative. In the final version some of these ellipses disappear. Others find their way into the dialogue as ways to indicate that people are thinking, usually pausing around the issue of difference, or affects of shame, concern, or embarrassment. The ellipses that remain in the narration allow Shori to express disbelief (e.g., that her antagonists consider themselves victims), concern (e.g., that the council would also judge her), or shame (e.g., that she was too rough when feeding from a symbiont). In addition, the spirit of the ellipses surfaces in the form of rhetorical questions. Shori asks herself multiple questions about how she will take care of her symbionts, how she will fight her enemies, how she will survive. The style sheet created for *Fledgling* indicated that there were several "suspension points," ellipses that ought not be changed to preserve the integrity of the novel.[62]

All of these ellipses do double duty as a way to demonstrate Shori's fatigue and confusion in the face of amnesia and to propel the action. They also aesthetically intervene in a genre (the vampire novel) that Butler critiqued for being long on explanation, short on plot.[63] The amnesia here uproots the general actionless plot that Butler worked against in her creation of *Fledgling* since she implored herself to inject explanation with action.[64] What aids her in this enterprise is the amnesia. Shori's disability, particularly because it reduces the ability to get inside her head, thwarts the interior availability typical of first-person narration and limits the explanations germane to vampire stories. It is worth noting that Butler experimented with making the entire novel a third-person narrative. In the beginning drafts of *Fledgling* she struggled to create a narrative voice in the third person that would adequately express Shori's confusion. The ellipses and rhetorical questions exploit and thwart the expectation that a first-person novel provides complete interiority and emotional availability. Since the novel mobilizes the ellipses to punctuate emotional reactions, it upends the idea that one requires grammatical or narrative cohesion to depict interiority.

Butler challenges the narrative cohesion expected of the genre of the novel as well. Her gaps and silences disrupt the wholeness we have come to expect of the genre. Certainly, the postmodern novel troubles that idea, marked as it is by fragmentation. However, the fragments of a postmodern novel can push toward coherence or resolution, whereas Butler's work tends toward remaining unresolved. Her characters' silences do more than demonstrate their hesitation around issues of difference, and the instability prompted by the presence of difference in a world hostile to it. Again, at the level of syntax, Butler disrupts the narrative. When Shori first meets the Gordons, they question her alongside Wright. When asked about the motive behind the attacks on Shori, Wright conjectures about Ina racists. Shori notes that "the younger ones listened, indifferent, but the older ones didn't much like what he was saying. It seemed to make them uncomfortable, embarrassed."[65] The following sentence appears after this statement: "Human racism meant nothing to the Ina because human races meant nothing to them."[66] In two drafts, this sentence appears within the narration as Shori's explanation for the Gordons' hesitancy.[67] In the final version, this statement is attributed to one of the fathers, but without quotation marks. Butler paid close attention to where quotation marks appeared as evidenced by the style sheet and her handwritten notes. Pulling the sentence out of the narration and attributing it to a specific Gordon removes the sentence from being a matter of Shori's interpretation. Leaving out the quotation marks also troubles the idea of whether that statement's sentiment should be attributed solely to one Gordon or to more. So, it is not filtered through Shori as part of the narration, but is also not solely in the mouth of one Gordon. The Gordons' discomfort with and denial of racism dovetails with the sentiments of Shori's antagonists, who connect her with a history of enslavement. The silence occasioned by the Gordons' liberalism cannot cover up oppressive ideology. It remains, invaginating the text. Butler's narrative demonstrates, through its fragmentation and silences, the effects of Blackness and madness in the text's aesthetic.

To be clear, Butler's aesthetic intervention does not exclusively exist in the ideological spaces of syntax and punctuation. One of the rules of science fiction is that the world the author creates must abide by its own internal logic. Within the world of *Fledgling*, part of the internal logic is the history of the Ina people. Though Butler does not break the rule insisting on an internal logic, she does not abide by the idea that the characters must be aware of the internal logic to which they abide. That is, the Gordons' liberalism and silence and the antagonists' hatred and genocide are two sides of the same narrative coin. They each participate in an act of historiographical revision, changing their past relationship to disability and Blackness by excising them. Unlike the critical impulse that permits representational detective work to recuperate Black disabled bodies and experiences, they cannot recuperate that which they do not think they have lost. They cannot treat as radical that which they considered so abject so as to not exist at all. Butler's text intervenes in the narrative logic that assumes the accepted stories about Ina origin and history are complete without the input of either the present or purported anomalies from the past. Ina construct the absence of Blackness and madness as a ballast of their identity ab ovo. The Gordons do not want to admit to the idea of Ina racists. They do not want to deal with the reality that Ina can be gravely mentally injured. (In point of fact, Shori's father, Iosif, is the only Ina who acknowledges that her head injury could be part of Ina experience.) Racism and ableism exert differing pressures on Ina history and ontology. Each destabilizes the Ina's notion of self, such that their only recourse is denial. To embrace the presence of racism in that moment would be to admit the possibility of dishonor and to more heavily court embarrassment and shame regarding Ina history or identity. To think about Ina injury, particularly amnesia, troubles the overarching paradigm they have developed for discussing their relationship to illness. Most often, they think in terms of physical disabilities, usually temporary injury that can be rectified, such as broken bones or pierced flesh. Here, Shori's amnesia upsets their understanding of themselves as generally sound—in relation to humans superlative—in mind and body. The absence of a possibility for cure destabilizes an aspect of themselves they consider fundamental—memory as tied to their longevity and as a necessary tool for their survival. Since mutual constitution occasions the recuperation of Blackness and madness, they would be absorbed in their history or origin stories but not normalized based on abjection. According to these Ina, they were not present to be absorbed at all. This historiographical maneuver implies that madness and Blackness have and create separate historical trajectories which, when combined with a history that insists on whiteness and ability, is destructive to their sense of self.

By muddying history, Butler allows Black madness to shift one of the hallmarks of science fiction: the audacity to imagine the future. The attempted genocide and the rhetoric of erasure push toward creating a bare life for Shori. Agamben develops the concept of bare life to account for those who exist between *zoe* (mere life) and *bios* (good life) and whose existence is included as a part of the Western cultural landscape but occluded from visual representation or polite conversation. Moreover, those with bare lives lose their rights as citizens, and their existence is limned by their fungibility. Alexander Weheliye revises this concept to think through the Middle Passage instead of the Muselmann of the Holocaust, remarking that other bodies in the Western world are also susceptible to bare lives. In Weheliye's revision, the bare lives to which Black people become susceptible are made possible by their de facto and long-standing position of fungibility vis-à-vis the state.[68] In Shori's case, the possibility remains that bare life becomes affixed to her Black amnesiac body not simply by virtue of genocidal action but also because of the accepted idea that the Ina exist outside the confines of race and racialization discourses.

In thinking through Shori's Black madness as variation rather than aberration, the text opens the space for Shori to display certain kinds of agency, loosen the hold of a bare life. Yet because her allies have to advocate for her to be considered Ina, I am hesitant to ascribe to Shori's Black madness an agentive quality. That is, how far away from a bare life can she be if her existence must be consistently justified before their Council of Judgment, and even then not fully decided or accepted? Black madness remains a provocation. Even as it forms the locus for the invagination of their history and the fold of their future, it both allows for agency and forecloses it. Black madness remains a wrinkle in the linear progression of history and time because of its opposition to their dominant ideology. As a result, it cannot have anything but a vexed agency, nor can it create itself outside the confines of a bare life. Moreover, Black madness, given its loss of time (amnesia) and aversion to time (changing the narrative) shifts the possibility of recuperation as a form of agency. Linked as it is to a bare life, affixed in history as such, it cannot fully recuperate its past nor rewrite the history to tell its story from its perspective.

Such a vexed position extends into the future. In terms of the narrative, Shori faces the dangers of the sexualized gaze and, possibly, antagonists deciding to avenge their families and harm Shori in the sequel. In Butler's notes, she implores herself to show children as part of the Ina community.[69] This nods to the characters' sense of a future even if that future is thwarted. Narratologically and aesthetically, the future poses a problem in the presence of Black madness. To be blunt, bare lives aren't afforded a future in the sense of progeny. As Alison Kafer describes, disability in the present portends "a future that bears too many traces of the ills of the present to be desirable. In this framework, a future with disability is a future no one wants, and the figure of the disabled person, especially the disabled fetus or child, becomes the symbol of this undesired future."[70] The future for Black mad subjects is a quagmire, and the struggle to represent it foregrounds the folds already present in the present and in the past. It is not merely that the future is unknowable or uncertain, but rather that it is unfathomable without the negotiation of ideological confines that create the past. The future tends to assume a possible solution—especially within a novel. Instead, this Black mad future assumes ideological conflict: the Black mad future is not fathomable because its present and its past are unclear.

Loosely, we have the contours and confines of Black madness. It is mutually constituted in historical terms but cannot be adequately delineated by projects that recuperate its presence or celebrate it as radical. The presence of Black madness allows for a partial unmaking of the logics that govern the linear progressive idea of time and space. Blackness and madness discomfort and confuse, particularly in intimate spaces where their cleaving is not possible. Though this subject position allows for agency, it also remains affixed to a bare life, holding in abeyance the critical possibilities of a freedom and a failure that is always on its way.

:: CONVERSATION 2

A MAD BLACK THANG

bleed dribble leak ooze seep splash trickle drop
character class grade make species variety form
audible lucid coherent distinct plain precise clear
canyon cut gap gorge path opening ravine pass
airy buoyant delicate feathery unsubstantial light
emit radiate diffuse spray spread scatter cast

—EVIE SHOCKLEY, "clare's song," *the new black*

I wish to pull a thread from the previous conversation. Recall that mutual
constitution—withal it promises to bring race and disability together—
tends toward two reading strategies that do not fully honor the complexities of the multiability, interracial encounter. Historicizing projects assume
linear progressive narratives in which Blacks and whites occupy the same
temporal plane; recuperative projects require Black disabled bodies to bear
up under the weight of white redemption. Octavia E. Butler's work theorizes
that this encounter requires reading strategies that attend to the uneven parameters of time and space and question the pressure on the Black mad subject to exist in service of others. Since this project is a series of conversations,
the next question to ask might be about what happens when we enter the intraracial encounter. That is, what happens when madness is a Black thang?[1]

The intraracial encounter poses its own problems for Black madness.
Though not exclusively writing about intraracial dynamics, Lennard Davis's
writing and Michelle Jarman's analysis of Billy Ray Johnson reveal, "When-

ever race and disability come together . . . ethnicity tends to be considered so much the 'stronger' category that disability disappears altogether."[2] That would lead us to believe that there is no analytic where disability, broadly, or madness, more specifically, can exist within a Black context. However, Black vernacular speech reveals a variety of euphemisms that describe madness, whether referring to mental illness, cognitive disability, or the perception of either one (i.e., touched, special, not right, in one's right mind, etc.). Further, the historical distrust between medical personnel and Black communities tends to calcify an intracultural dictum that disability be taken care of within families or local enclaves. Disability, writ large, and madness in particular occupy a fraught space within Black cultural contexts: marked by the simultaneity of erasure, vexed presence, and protection.

As I mentioned, I deploy the term madness because of the critical possibilities it offers in its vagueness. It operates as a way to describe impairments such as cognitive disability or mental illness as well as a catchall phrase designed to reference those not behaving according to culturally prescribed norms. Here, I harken back to the idea that madness is maddeningly everywhere with biopsychological and sociocultural valences. Within Black cultural contexts, madness not only has this critical purchase but also carries with it the vernacular appeal of excess (e.g., mad as equivalent to very) and anger. For the purposes of this discussion, I loosely bifurcate madness into two categories, keeping in mind that each carries with it the cultural valences of excess: cognitive impairment (read: autism, Down syndrome, traumatic brain injury, dementia, etc.) and mental illness (read: bipolar, depression, schizophrenia, etc.). I split these experiences in order to attend to the differences in the way madness writ large is treated within Black cultural contexts.[3] There are overlapping concerns, to be sure, but the reactions within Black communities shift depending on the particular kind of madness one demonstrates. Lurking within each discussion of madness— cognitive impairment or mental illness—is the idea, simply put, that Blackness changes things. A Black cultural context mandates a different set of interpretive strategies because of the confluence of structural racism from the outside and its impact on the intracultural community, and structural patriarchy and ableism emanating from within the community. Parsing mental illness and cognitive disability allows for a certain type of granularity when discussing Black cultural contexts and madness.

The conversation that follows relocates the discussion of Blackness and madness outside the confines of the interracial encounter in order to understand what may constitute disability cultures within Blackness. What analytics become necessary when examining madness within Blackness? There are of course two caveats to this discussion. First, it is not entirely possible to get outside the confines of white cisheteropatriarchy, since it structures so much of what is possible within Black contexts. For that reason, I turn to Nalo Hopkinson's work because she dares to theorize a set of Black cultural contexts that are largely independent from white cisheteropatriarchal structures. Hopkinson's theorizing about intraracial contexts relies on the particular tools of Black speculative fiction, even though her ideas resonate outside of that creative context.[4] I also focus on cultural narratives because of what they offer in terms of theorizing from below, especially since "through analysis, texts on disability can be made to reveal the texture of community life."[5] The second caveat is that there are a wide variety of Black cultural contexts available to examine. The intention of this discussion is not to provide a rubric that suits all of them but to provide an inroad to examination, one that exists as a set of overarching analytical possibilities until others develop. As a way to develop this schema, I read the current strategies for discussing madness within Blackness. Again, the critical literature reveals itself to itself through the gaps it leaves unattended. I propose the mad Black as a way to reimagine and reread. Nalo Hopkinson, as an artist-theorist, creates mad Black characters—one with a cognitive disability and another with a mental illness—in her mad Black novel *Midnight Robber* (2000). The two narratives twin each other and open up the possibilities for interpreting madness within Black communities.

Show, (Im)Prove

In considering mental illness within Black communities, two interpretive moments in the critical literature open up the parameters to think through how madness lays bare common culturally accepted narratives about Blackness. For example, in Anna Mollow's meditation on Meri Nana-Ama Danquah's *Willow Weep for Me: A Black Woman's Journey through Depression, A Memoir* (1998), Mollow concludes that Danquah's narrative of depression foregrounds her race, class position, and immigrant status as a barrier to receiving adequate health care for her depression. Contrary to most within the ex-patient/survivor/consumer movement, Danquah's concern is not overmedication or forced medication but a lack thereof. Not only do health care professionals demonstrate a lack of competence in discussing the influence of racial discrimination on Danquah's depression, but Danquah also has to combat the following ideas: that depression is not real, that she is particularly strong as a Black woman, and (specific to her identity as an immigrant) that she only need work harder to overcome her sadness. Mollow reads Danquah's narrative as a structural critique of the medical establishment's tendency to ignore and/or underestimate Black women's pain. I would add that Danquah's memoir is a cultural critique of intraracial dictums that diminish Black women's experiences with mental illness. What Mollow's reading reveals is that Danquah's depression exceeds the parameters in which she is expected to operate as a Ghanaian immigrant woman in the United States, parameters set by both dominant cultures and her own. To my mind, Danquah becomes circumscribed by her inability to appropriately perform the scripts of Black womanhood because of her mental illness. Here, the critical gap lies in the space between how Danquah's depression indexes structural critique and how it also points to sociocultural critique.

Whereas Mollow's reading of Danquah's narrative reveals how structural racism materially compounds the assault of oppressive intracultural narratives, literary interpretations within African American Studies unmask the limited space available for Black characters who experience madness. When discussing August Wilson's oeuvre, which includes his cadre of cognitively disabled characters, Harry Elam describes "racialized madness" as a "trope that became operative in clinical practice, literary creation, and cultural theory in the modern period as artists, critics, and practitioners in all these arenas identified social and cultural roots for Black psychological impairment."[6] Elam usefully locates this trope in Frantz Fanon's and W. E. B. Du Bois's work as a diagnosis of what ails African descended people. The solution with August Wilson's (and others') work is to upend the social, cultural, and discursive elements that comprise a world hostile to Blackness. Elam argues that August Wilson creates characters that experience madness to clarify how much social and spiritual change would be necessary for a group of people who have already been driven mad by a mad world. This is a sociogenic madness, madness without pathos.[7] I reference Elam and his work in African American literary study because of the way sociogenic theories have particular critical purchase for this field. They denounce the pathologization of Black people for being Black yet embrace the understanding of the world as anti-Black. Yet, this is also madness without the multidimensionality that accompanies embodiment or aesthetic intervention: madness in service of sanity.[8]

Mollow, Elam, and others abide by one delimited script: madness is not a biological or psychosocial impairment with experiences all its own. Rather, those who are Black and mad are societal bellwethers. Their madness either presages or pinpoints putative larger issues at stake. This idea rests on the politicization of both Blackness and madness, where either or both are primarily or solely political identities. Black madness then becomes revelatory for the rest of the world and the Black mad folks—real or imagined—stand in for an examination of what is happening. Their existence functions as an analysis *tout court*, an *explication de texte* that the world operates according to anti-Black logics. This script is of course not new. We have consistently thought of people who occupy marginalized social positions as markers of whether our governments, cultures, and communities fulfill ethical or moral obligations of caretaking. However, we cannot completely shunt aside the way the idea of a societal bellwether objectifies and distances the Black mad, stripping them of the multidimensionality that would emerge within a communal context. Critics attend to this conceptual problem by considering these characters or people within intraracial communities, but often these communities embrace this script as well. From this critical impulse follows the erroneous idea that the Black mad do not have community, or they operate as lone soldiers. Here, their existential or ontological homelessness becomes a vehicle for other (sometimes, non-Black or non-mad) characters or people to discover their own missing humanity. Or, said homelessness results in death.

Read in the fold, in the break. The Black mad as societal bellwether moves according to a linear progression of time, where their existence must be incorporated or excised in order to demonstrate progress of some sort. (Billy Ray Johnson echoes here.) Typically, that results in an erasure of either their Blackness or their madness. Removing the impulse to view the Black mad as living analyses, they become invaginated into the moments of a text and do not function in the service of others but rather have their own plotlines and, sometimes, create their own resolutions. Or don't. Narrative time no longer stands still, but it also does not operate strictly in linear fashion, preferring to intussuscept itself or create gaps and pauses.

Sight of the Unseen

Narratives about people of color with cognitive disabilities are difficult to come by, generally speaking.[9] The largest stumbling block is the issue of representation: who represents whom, and where those representations occur. There have been some popular representations of Black people with cognitive disabilities, most recently celebrity mothers of autistic children. This cadre of mothers includes famed R&B chanteuse Toni Braxton, actress Holly Robinson Peete, and actress and singer Tisha Campbell-Martin. Their work largely focuses on advocacy for their children. On the occasions when their children do speak (usually within the context of reality television), they tend to voice overcoming narratives. Largely, these tellings rely on the idea that the cognitive disability is an invisible one, which poses trouble because it is not readily understood as disability. The resulting misunderstandings, bullying, or trauma stems from the unrecognizability of these illnesses. These narratives fall in line, culturally speaking, with the arguments of those of Nirmala Erevelles, Allison Carey, and Michael Bérubé, who all agree that the repercussion of announcing oneself or being identified as cognitively disabled is a loss of citizenship rights. Here, the rights are not merely material but can also include cultural capital.

Invisibility surfaces as a long-standing component of stories about Blacks with cognitive disabilities. During the antebellum period, slaveholders could demand compensation for supposedly unfit slaves. Within the critical literature, the understanding of physical and mental fitness are combined not only because slaves were not thought to be particularly intelligent but also because mental fitness was a necessary component in some assessments of physical labor. So-called soundness of mind was determined by a confluence of physical and mental conditions such as "skin color, gender, character, vice, health, body, and emotional state."[10] One of the characteristics of fitness was a degree of mental acuity (which slavers were likely to miss upon initial inspection of the human property) and a characteristic for which slavers could demand compensation. Successful litigation often depended on the slaver's ability to prove that the human property was unable to perform the duties for which it was purchased. Most important for these discussions is that the litigation occurred after sales were made, indicating that slavers were expected to have recourse to legal action for impairments that were not visible at the time of purchase. In this paradigm, one's worth as a Black person with a cognitive impairment—no matter its imaginary quality—is determined by one's production. Such possibilities for legal action created a link between the mental acuity of enslaved persons, invisibility, and profit.

This connection appears in the discourse regarding rehabilitation in the early twentieth century as well. The historical record conflates physical ability and mental ability as a way to disenfranchise Blacks economically.

Here, I mine the gaps in critical literature similarly to my earlier discussion of Rosemarie Garland Thomson. Black World War I veterans contended with rehabilitation policies that "devalued, deskilled, and institutionalized [them] and dismissed their claims to rehabilitation as spurious attempts to unjustly profit from their 'natural inferiority.'"[11] Rather than review their claims as disabilities acquired during military service, officials delegitimized Black veterans' need for rehabilitation by ascribing their disabilities to venereal disease and tuberculosis, which were, again according to officials, endemic to the race. This rhetoric built upon the idea of Blackness itself as a congenital, cognitive defect (further conflating physical ailment with cognitive impairment). The result was the removal of some veterans from the communities to which they may have contributed and of which they were definitely a part. When these veterans were denied rehabilitation, they were also denied the opportunity to earn a living in the postwar labor economy. Here, the connection between mental acuity, invisibility, and profit arises again. This time, the putative defect of Blackness gives rise to an imagined and invisible cognitive impairment that circumscribes the availability of economic self-determination.

Though cognitive impairment is not, strictly speaking, emblazoned on the flesh, it nevertheless subtends interaction as a structuring presence. The conception about worth, particularly related to capitalist profit and economic viability, becomes imbricated in the narratives about cognitive disability. Entangled here, enfolded here, are legibility, visibility, economic viability, and cognitive disability. On the one hand, cognitive disability and the rhetoric thereof are marshaled as a way to justify exclusion from resources. On the other hand, cognitive disability becomes visible when one cannot prove one's worth or value to the labor economy. In either case, cognitive disability remains wedded to its legibility as an identity category, regardless of whether it is linked to other categories (Blackness itself). One reads cognitive disability based on interaction within a community regardless of whether that cognitive disability has a diagnosis attached. Such a reading may be complicated by the shifting terrain of legibility, determined as it is by cultural expectation, social convention, and medical narratives about cognition. Of interest to this conversation is how observation and visibility rests at the crux of these ideas: namely, one believes that one can judge, ascertain, and observe cognitive disability at work. The stare, despite its interrogative heft, is incomplete.[12] The problem is that these understandings operate with ocularity as the central sensory praxis despite the fact that legibility is not determined by sight, neither singularly nor primarily. Cognitive disability disrupts sight as having exclusive critical purchase over interpretation.

Enter the Mad Black

Considering Black cultural contexts where mental illness and cognitive disability occur, the two major Western modes of interpretation—ocularity and (drawing on our earlier conversation) linear time—no longer retain the exclusive right to interpret meaning. The Black mad are, in some sense, no more. They become the mad Black. I theorize mad Black and mad Blackness as a formulation that disrupts the ocular and linear legacies of the West's conception of space and time, respectively. To theorize the concept of the mad Black or mad Blackness opens up critical space to consider how the discourses of madness and Blackness not only operate in intraracial spaces but also intensify and dismantle common understandings of each other. When mad becomes a modifier for Black it carries with it the charge of excess (i.e., more Black, really Black, unapologetically Black, Blackity Black), anger, and insanity as it simultaneously functions as an intensifier for Blackness itself. In some ways, madness amplifies Blackness in this conception, pushing it to excess, but it also has the potential to dismantle it. Said potential lies precisely in the disruption of Western space and time. Sight no longer acts as the dominant mode of sense making. Linear progressions of time no longer capture the movement of subjects and objects through narrative. Mad Blackness fills in the gaps heretofore created by reading strategies (i.e., mutual constitution) that rely on these two Western modalities of interpretation. For instance, Octavia E. Butler's mad Black character cleaves time from space with her very existence, such that the linear progressive narrative plane is disrupted. She also foregrounds the lie in thinking of the impeachability of sight as the dominant mode of interpretation. Her allies cannot see her illness. Their understanding based on sight—no matter its superlative quality— is impoverished.

The mad Black then is not solely disruptive because of its embodiment. But also, the mad Black figure and mad Blackness stage a narratological intervention in how we analyze and tell stories about race and disability writ large. Mad Blackness describes the aesthetics of a text that refuses to adhere to ocularcentrism or linearity. In these texts—including but not limited to the ones in these conversations—madness and Blackness pervade the structure of the text such that linear renderings of the narrative always

A Mad Black Thang 57

do a disservice to the text and an emphasis on sight forecloses interpretive possibility. To be clear, it is not that ocularcentrism and linearity are wholly inappropriate, but rather that they are explicitly incomplete due to the influence of madness and Blackness in the structure and characters of the text. As a result, mad Blackness necessarily critiques texts that denigrate madness or Blackness or both.

Despite, and perhaps owing to, this disruptive quality, I would not define mad Blackness as a revolutionary force, nor would I expect mad Black figures to offer solutions. Their disruption—of interpretation, of narrative—does not require that they provide solutions, since that contrasts their suspicion of linearity and teleology, nor does it require that they be benevolent, since that often requires they be in service of those that create and maintain anti-Black ableist and sanist structures. This book, *Black Madness :: Mad Blackness*, is one such example of a mad Black text. As I mentioned, the conversations herein reveal critical conversations to themselves, and seek to perturb some of the foundations upon which Black studies and disability studies rest all while yoking them irrevocably together.

Nalo Hopkinson's work in *Midnight Robber* (2000) theorizes this concept through her two mad Black figures (one who experiences mental illness and another, cognitive impairment) and her aesthetic commentary on narrative structure. *Midnight Robber* is not her only novel that explores the mad Black. Hopkinson's oeuvre includes a variety of characters and plotlines influenced by or experiencing some form of madness peculiar to the worlds they inhabit. In *Sister Mine* (2013), one of Hopkinson's main characters has a congenital magic defect. In *The Chaos* (2012), the entire world randomly changes so that rules of physics, metaphysics, climate, thermodynamics, and electricity no longer apply. *Brown Girl in the Ring* (1998) features a cadre of characters who do not share the reality of the community. *The New Moon's Arms* (2007) wades into the territory of madness within a subplot about the main character's origins. Hopkinson's short stories in *Skin Folk* (2001), particularly "Tawny Bitch," which depicts a woman in an asylum, also feature (and I mean that in the vernacular sense) mad Black characters and aesthetics.[13] For the characters for whom this is an embodied reality, madness can be real or imagined. It tends to divide into the two categories described and parsed above: cognitive disability and mental illness. Cognitive impairment within the world of Hopkinson's novels carries with it a sense of responsibility to the person experiencing the impairment. Those who have been perceived as having mental illness tend to be sequestered or isolated from a larger community either physically or emotionally. Determining soundness of mind crystallizes in our logophilic obsession with the book and the insistence on the unimpeachability of sight. Here—in this break—is where Nalo Hopkinson's work becomes instructive.

In Hopkinson's second novel, *Midnight Robber*, she creates a mad Black text with mad Black characters, two sisters. One, Quamina, has what might be called a cognitive impairment, and the other, Tan-Tan, develops what might be termed a mental health concern. The two sisters' narratives double each other by providing a set of interpretive strategies for understanding how madness functions in (a) Black community. *Midnight Robber* takes place on a planet settled by the Marryshow Corporation with a majority pan-Caribbean population. The settlement itself is a place of leisure where few people perform physical labor and most are connected to artificial intelligence called Granny Nanny from birth. The only exception is a group of people who choose to remain disconnected and own a cab service that they operate on foot. The cuckolded (and adulterous) mayor, Antonio, after killing his wife's lover with a poisoned blade, leaves his town of Toussaint and kidnaps his daughter, Tan-Tan, along the way. They escape to a prison colony called New Half-Way Tree. Upon arrival, they meet Chichibud, a douen (packbird animal), who guides them through the wilderness to a village, Junjuh Town. The doctor of that village is one of Antonio's former mistresses, who has, since being exiled, given birth to Antonio's child (and Tan-Tan's half sister), Quamina. Quamina lives with cognitive impairments as a result of her journey from Toussaint to New Half-Way Tree. Antonio and Tan-Tan learn that life on New Half-Way Tree requires the physical labor that Toussaint eradicated. It is in their new home where Antonio begins to repeatedly rape Tan-Tan starting on her ninth birthday. After seven years of abuse, Tan-Tan kills Antonio during his final sexual attack when he impregnates her. She runs away from her village, settling with the packbird douen animals who are native to New Half-Way Tree. They shelter her until she betrays the secret of where they live, after which they excommunicate her. She and her adopted packbird sister, Abitefa, must survive in the forest until Abitefa can find another douen home and Tan-Tan a human settlement. Eventually, Tan-Tan decides to settle down in a new village with her childhood friend-*cum*-partner. The novel ends with Tan-Tan giving birth to Antonio's child.

Nalo Hopkinson creates Quamina as a cognitively disabled character, which allows Hopkinson to raise several questions about madness within intraracial communities. I realize that calling Quamina cognitively disabled appears to perform a critic's sleight of hand by vaguely diagnosing her (blasphemous within disability studies circles) or pathologizing her (blasphemous within Black studies circles). My rationale for such irreverence creeps along the edge of both disciplinary boundaries, harnessing disability studies' propensity for uncovering moments of disability and impairment regardless of whether it is named as such, and Black studies' focus on processes of racialization that determine how one is treated. I refer to Quamina as cognitively disabled because of the way Hopkinson's narrative limns her difference. She is called bassourdie, for instance, which takes on the double valence of foolish or stupid and crazy, making it synonymous with the pejorative retard. The references to Quamina's incontinence, and her short declarative sentences infantilize her—a common tropological nod to the cognitively disabled.[14]

In a novel that Hopkinson herself, in interviews and with the epigraphs, describes as "in part *about* language,"[15] particularly language that "[reveals] the rotten roots of some of our ideas,"[16] Quamina's silence complicates the role of the sonic such that not talking is not equal to not speaking. Quamina has very little language of her own but does engage in the way the other characters do. To be fair, Quamina receives about as much interiority as any of the characters that aren't Tan-Tan, keeping in mind that the novel is written from the perspective of a limited third-person narrator. Though Hopkinson marks her as a nonrhetor in a world full of rhetors, this difference of silence does not exclude her from the narrative's world making. Quamina's cognitive disability occupies a vexed space between radicality and stereotype. *Midnight Robber* suggests that Quamina occupies a space similar to that of autistic characters (that are not savants) who are thought to be largely uncommunicative and desirous of solitude. (Note that Quamina's character demonstrates no predilection for solitude.) I would argue that Hopkinson's choice to limit Quamina's speech forces an expansion of how we interact with language in a novel. Silence forms its own narrative. Quamina's silence does not automatically indicate a silencing by the author or the text or even an indictment of the silence forced upon her by others' weddedness to spoken language. In fact, her silence may also be in keeping with the desire to render her Blackness with a sense of quiet, a way of pushing against the idea that Blackness is always loud, emphatic, or auditory.[17] What if the silence was not indicative of unknowability, working against the metaphorical meanings associated with Blackness or cognitive disability as an unbreachable chasm? What if the silence solicited a narratological form of respect, tapping into but also sidestepping the alignment of madness with genius?

In mad Black terms, Hopkinson's depiction of Quamina disrupts how we tell stories about speech, specifically the common understanding of non-rhetors as evidence of a life that is a "limit without possibility."[18] Consider together Melanie Yergeau's "autie-ethnographic narrative" and Stuart Murray's *Representing Autism* (2008), which both trouble the depiction of autistic subjects as nonrhetors, incapable of using language and understanding affect. Murray and Yergeau offer a way to read Hopkinson's silence through Quamina and not about her (or the others for whom she may serve as fictional analogue). Murray writes about his partiality and positionality as a caregiver for his autistic child, noting that he must "[shuttle] back and forth between these various positions—subjective engagement and critical distance."[19] As a result, he recognizes that "to talk of characters with autism in fiction is not simply to engage in some simple process of spotting" but rather that "it is possible to see autism reordering the narratives in which it is found, giving stresses and inflections to responses that might [*sic*] familiar and as a consequence quite possibly [change] their meaning altogether."[20] Yergeau's narrative—which includes an involuntary commitment to a psychiatric ward—reminds us of the violent dangers inherent in the impulse to designate autistic people as devoid of language. Sardonically, she asks, "How can one have autism and have something to say?"[21] Reading Yergeau and Murray alongside Quamina (staving off the impulse to diagnose her specifically as autistic) allows Hopkinson's narrative to rebut the idea that communication requires speech or stasis to be intelligible. Through Quamina, silence reorders the text not as evidence of lack or of unknowability but rather another iteration of interaction. In other words, Quamina reflects that "there might be ways of productively using silence and nonverbal means of communication: in short, language that is not considered 'language' by the dominant culture."[22] Even in Black communities where the colonizer's tongue poses a problem, immediate recourse to the tongue of the colonized may foreclose the possibilities of silence. Must Caliban always speak? What this particular character's silence foregrounds is the extent to which silences appear in other portions of the novel. That is, how do we interpret the communal silence around Antonio's philandering in Toussaint or his abuse of Tan-Tan in New Half-Way Tree? What of the silences created by the limitations of the written word to express the sounds of the packbirds? Silence then cannot denote that Quamina (or characters like her) are deficient in language. It is simply that silence is a part of the language they must use, especially when the other option is not speech per se but the written word.

Another (limited) reading would be to understand Quamina's silence as metaphorical for the willful communal reserve around Antonio's abusive patriarchal behavior: philandering, abuse of power, kidnapping, rape. Though Quamina would gain critical purchase as a symbol, this reading would delimit how we could read her as part of the story's action. Recall that the mad Black does not exist in service of others, and mad Black interpretive strategies do not propose to neatly account for these characters. Rather than read reductively, I push past the above idea to think about the complex relationship she foregrounds between communal coercion and Black patriarchy. Quamina is Antonio's child by Aislin, Tan-Tan's former nurse. Rather than face his responsibilities on Toussaint, Antonio banishes a pregnant Aislin to the penal colony of New Half-Way Tree. One critic describes Quamina as Aislin's "disfigured daughter,"[23] which indexes how Quamina came to be. Typically, disability studies analyses avoid conversations about the origins of disability since those narratives tend to privilege medical explanations about people rather than their own accounts. With nonrhetors, stories about origins tend to follow well-worn scripts that disregard the opinions and experiences of those who eventually become the object (not the subject) of the narrative.[24] Hopkinson's speculative fiction narrative provides an origin story regarding Quamina that challenges the impulse to think of her as metaphor, but still requires an engagement with the how of her disability. When one takes the trip "up New Half-Way Tree," one must pass through several "veils" in order to reach the new world, the new dimension, which causes significant bodily change. Since Aislin makes the journey while pregnant, Quamina's development is shaped by the physical transformations the veil prompts. Tan-Tan, for instance, describes the first shift, saying, "It was as though her belly was turning inside out, like wearing all her insides on the outside."[25] During the second veil, she "felt as though her tailbone could elongate into a tail, long and bald like a manicou rat's. Her cries of distress came out like hyena giggles. The tail tip twitched. She could feel how unfamiliar muscles would move the unfamiliar limb."[26] Though Tan-Tan soon becomes herself again, these olfactory and physical transformations mark her journey from citizen to exiled subject. The fact that Aislin has to make the trip at all demonstrates Antonio's power over the community of Toussaint. The penal system upholds his heteropatriarchal control and allows him to punish those who would reveal his secrets.

Quamina then becomes part of the physical evidence that marks Aislin's transition from citizen to exiled subject and, furthermore, evidence that the community collectively consents to her banishment. Quamina's impairment is the result of the power of Black cisheteropatriarchy, a clear reminder that impairment is politicized.[27]

Quamina's impairment indexes and challenges the aforementioned link between cognitive disability, citizenship, and (capitalist) productivity. Yet, the narratives about her impairment frustrate an easy alignment of worth and cognitive disability with physical labor and economic utility. I would be remiss if I did not point out that the previous examples relied on US-based histories and historical record. Hopkinson draws from a pan-Caribbean history of slavery deliberately. Since transatlantic slavery was a vast hemispheric project, the connection between capitalist profit, putative physical and mental fitness, and Blackness holds differently but remains intact. New Half-Way Tree, as a penal colony, seems to determine its understanding of citizenry based on physical labor, and Junjuh Town in particular adds to this the requirement of affability. Through Quamina, Hopkinson forces any interpretation of Quamina—from characters within the story to critics reading it—to grapple with the ableist implications of such requirements. One-Eye, the default mayor of Junjuh Town in New Half-Way Tree, questions Quamina's existence, recapitulating eugenics logic: "I ain't know what Aislin make she live for. She only a burden."[28] One-Eye's lover and friend Claude chastens him by describing Quamina's contributions to their community: "Quamina quiet, and she sweet, and she does help Aislin round the place."[29] In short, Quamina earns her keep like the rest of the exiled, and, in point of fact, she contributes more. Claude's commentary about her contribution signals that it is not only her assistance that marks her utility but also her demeanor. In other words, he refuses to discount her or her contributions because of her neuroatypicality. Quamina then is not a problem to be solved in the way Tan-Tan intimates she would be on Toussaint (i.e., "Why didn't they just fix her?") but rather a contributor to the larger, valued trade of medicine and, just as important for Claude, the peaceful communal atmosphere.

There are two potential red flags for this reading: first, Quamina's citizenship (according to Claude) rests on her ability to perform a putative good cripple identity; and, second, her association with medicine appears to confirm that impairment must be fixed. Yet, Quamina as mad Black leaves these interpretations elliptically open, thwarting their potential ableism and racism, even while providing no interpretive (re)solution. Certainly, Claude's comment engages with ableist eugenics logic that would require the cognitively disabled to earn their keep via affective labor. Nevertheless, the complicated depiction of Quamina's character intimates that the novel itself does not endorse this point of view. Rather, it lays out Claude's idea next to those of One-Eye and Tan-Tan, such that they are part of a set of reactions this community has vis-à-vis cognitive disability. Leaving open this line of thinking should also illuminate how cognitive disability functions within a Black community. Claude, One-Eye, and Tan-Tan clarify that ableism is not merely a problem of interracial encounter. In this way, Hopkinson allows Quamina to delimit one of the boundaries of mad Blackness: namely, that it cannot, nor should it be expected to be proxy for radicality.[30] If one considers Quamina's relationship to medicine solely in her capacity as medical assistant, then her job to facilitate the cures of others might indicate an inclination to fix people rather than deal with disability. However, Quamina's origins frustrate that idea. Her birth signifies on the disruption of space and time that is the penal colony and the so-called free space, Toussaint, from which they are exiled. The circumstances of her birth elucidate that stories on Toussaint have gaps, and distortions as a direct result of Black heteropatriarchy. So, her cognitive difference reminds everyone that their adherence to and heralding of a linear progression of time and first-order causal logic (if this, then that) is a choice. That is, Quamina's embodiment indicates that the entire penal colony (and Toussaint) must reckon with disability either through an assiduous and violent policing of it (Toussaint) or its presence as a complex reminder of that violence (New Half-Way Tree).

Quamina's relationship to medicine is not solely through the origins of her disability but also through the interactions her cognition facilitates. Hopkinson chooses to trouble the medicalized notion of disability by challenging the way it rests on a strict bifurcation between human and animal. That is, disability gets discussed and thought of as a condition to avoid because it places humans on par with animals. Cognitive disability in particular gets configured as a condition that dehumanizes. Mel Chen's *Animacies* pinpoints how dehumanization requires the making of an object and the unmaking of a subject.[31] Chen illumes how such a making/unmaking occurs on a semantic level: "Language users use animacy hierarchies to manipulate, affirm, and shift the ontologies that matter in the world."[32] Hopkinson places this association before us regarding Quamina by discussing her incontinence, then upends this logic because it is the douen packbird animals that provide medication. Claude says, "She couldn't learn to walk good, or talk; only wetting up sheself all the time . . . Asje my douen bring some bush tea for she. He tell Lin she must make Quamina drink a little every morning. Next thing you know, Quamina start to talk!"[33]

Since ableism is predicated on the idea that humanity requires certain fluencies in language and in body, it often requires a strict line between animals and humans. When ableism abets white supremacy, that line ceases to exist between certain animals and Black people (usually of the canine, simian and porcine variety). Here, Hopkinson worries that line by placing the intelligence regarding flora and fauna and their medicinal effects mostly in the claws of the douen. I sound a word of caution that the speculative fiction element here should not pigeonhole (and I use the animal reference deliberately) Hopkinson's work. Her use of the douen as a set of characters should foreground the dynamic kinship relationships already present between animals and humans including but not limited to the way animals act as medicinal (i.e., therapy dogs), the structuring of family relationships between animals and humans (i.e., cat mommies, dog families), and the equation of human and animal behavior (i.e., organizing college professors is like herding cats). Hopkinson's narrative resists the thingification characters ascribe to the douen (whom the humans derisively call ratbats), unmaking their ideas about human subjectivity. Unmaking here also extends beyond the confines of the text to cover, or uncover, or recover the association between Blackness and animacy. As Chen describes, the coercive nature of animacy's linguistic trapping is that it "consists of both mundane and exceptional reinforcements,"[34] one of which is the consistent association of Blackness with animacy. I hasten to add that Blackness's association with animacy undergirds the idea that disability and Blackness are synonymous. Worrying the line between humans and animals, then, reveals one of the mundane reinforcements of ableism: namely, that putative real humanity requires shunning a connection to animals. When Hopkinson troubles the line between Black humans and animals in particular, it might appear that she reaffirms Black dehumanization, but given the way she complicates ableism, she actually unmakes a definition of Blackness that places animacy-as-abjection at the crux of either racist ideology or an intraracial respectability politics.

Though Quamina disappears from narrative view once Tan-Tan flees Junjuh Town, Tan-Tan's narrative of mental illness doubles Quamina's such that both sisters' stories echo through the novel in its entirety.[35] In both narrative threads, reading madness makes legible the deleterious effects of Black patriarchy on both Toussaint and New Half-Way Tree, including the community's complicity and complacency regarding Antonio's sexual exploitation of Aislin and, later, Tan-Tan. For Quamina and Tan-Tan, the silences around their madness indicate the community's relationship, however vexed, to their madness. Origin narratives, of their respective madnesses—both related to Antonio's sexual abuse—require that the analytical tools become more capacious to portray how their impairments are the results of politicized, sexualized, and raced violence. Moreover, their relationship with the douen requires a paradigm shift regarding animacy. Here is where mad Blackness becomes useful as an interpretive strategy. It foregrounds the way both sisters are interpreted as excessive (even if that interpretation cannot hold) while providing the reading strategies necessary—suspicion of ocularcentrism and linearity—for understanding their potential to disrupt and structure the narrative.

Tan-Tan's narrative, since she becomes the loquacious Robber Queen, also operates as a foil to Quamina's. Of particular interest to me is Tan-Tan's putative healing near the final pages of the novel. I hesitate to describe these final pages as an ending per se because the novel itself suggests otherwise. (Octavia E. Butler echoes here.) In that scene, the interpretive possibilities of silence, and the unreliability of linearity culminate in Tan-Tan's experience at a fête, Carnival. She must retell her story: Antonio uses Tan-Tan to replace the wife he lost on Toussaint, Tan-Tan's emotionally absent mother, Ione. Antonio maps his simultaneous anger, lust, and disgust for Ione onto Tan-Tan such that she internalizes his feelings, alongside a belief in her own sexual power. The good and bad dichotomy plagues her even when she flees the town because she cannot place blame on Antonio, so fully has she absorbed his mixed emotions for her. Good Tan-Tan plays the "Robber Queen" in other parts of the colony, dispensing a kind of vigilante justice. She appears to reconcile herself once she participates in a Carnival fête, telling the story about her sexual abuse while playing the Robber Queen. After her story, she flees to the bush to give birth to Antonio's child with the help of her new partner, Melonhead, and her douen sister, Abitefa.

[When marked as insane and excised from community, the Black mad undergo erasure. In contrast, the mad Black can live inside the mistake of erasing either Blackness or madness, erring and preferring existence that disrupts the facility of celebration or abjection] Consider Tan-Tan's performance at the fête. Some critics choose to read Tan-Tan's performance and her delivery experience as a moment of reconciliation, celebration, and agency.[36] Indeed, the novel suggests that Tan-Tan feels better after the fête, and her delivery explains the new role of the artificial intelligence, Granny Nanny, interface. However, the fête and delivery experience creates some gaps in the story that trouble the reconciliation, or, more bluntly, ableist overcoming narrative and sanist interpretation.[37] In thinking through the reconciliation narrative in particular, this moment hinges on Tan-Tan's commitment to a linear narrative vis-à-vis her abuse. Instead, she condemns her community by pointing to the way their complicity disrupts the progression story that follows a clear through-line: She is kidnapped. She is raped. She is beaten. She kills Antonio. She flees. The community's knowledge (and specifically that of her stepmother) invaginates this story, not only providing her with the murder weapon (given to her by her stepmother) but also shifting the locus of responsibility from Tan-Tan or Antonio to the community of Junjuh Town. Rather than accept the community's ostracization, Tan-Tan inverts a familiar narrative in which "cultural concepts of irrationality and sexist norms of mental health marginalize people with mental illnesses in attacking their personhood."[38] Thinking beyond *Midnight Robber*, the overcoming narrative generally elides the import of supportive community, and mistakenly transforms structural inequality to a matter of individual obstacle. The reconciliation narrative in particular assumes that madness is individual aberration, rather than socially circumscribed where the boundaries of sanity are coercively policed. Her disruption of both allows her the space to maneuver inside a community that has made the mistake of being silent about her trauma.

Returning to Hopkinson's depiction of Tan-Tan's reprisal of the Robber Queen as an example of such disruption opens up the possibility of interpretation. Tan-Tan's final Robber Queen speech, as an act of mad Blackness, destabilizes the reach and definition of sanity, indicating that it is contingent upon the belief of others and the communal threshold for (sexualized) violence. Tan-Tan's speech may function as a kind of triumph for her, but it is not fixed. She switches into third person to describe her experience, continuing to enact the split personality that allows her to be the Robber Queen in the first place: "Someone in Tan-Tan's body took a breath, filled Tan-Tan's lungs with singing air spoke in her voice."[39] Though her use of vulgarity startles the participants ("Is she father who fuck she."[40]) and disrupts the storytelling usually associated with Carnival, it is not clear whether they believe her. One might diminish the import of onlookers' belief, but their buy-in (and their reasons for doing so) proves significant when thinking through the reach of her madness and its relationship to the particular culture of the community.[41] If they believe her, she is not insane based on the boundaries set up by the community. Tan-Tan's madness at Carnival then provides a vexed but useful easement into her cultural community. If they do not believe her, their disbelief may help solidify the seemingly bright line that separates those who are and are not considered sound of mind. Their disbelief would also ossify the community's complacency (and therefore complicity) with the Black patriarchal influence that drives Tan-Tan to this point. Skepticism would excise Tan-Tan again, relegating her to the bush, circumscribing her social network to her douen sister, and stripping her of the identity that allows participation in this community. At the end of the fête, members of the community occupy each of these positions—doubt, belief, awe—so all of these relationships to Tan-Tan exist at the same time: "Hanging on her every word the crowd was frozen, most in attitudes of horror, but a few just looked wary."[42] "People looked at Tan-Tan uncertainly. Some smiled. Many scowled. Somebody asked a friend, 'So is Masque that was or real?'"[43]

The end result of the fête is that Tan-Tan occupies a liminal place vis-à-vis her inclusion in the community and her putative mental illness. Though the text says that "now was time to put away guilt," it says nothing about the fact that, as Tan-Tan says, "Sorrow was my father, my mother. I know sorrow good."[44] The two statements, the former in narration and the latter in quotation, indicate that Tan-Tan's time as Robber Queen may be over, but her trauma and possible mental illness remain. Shortly after the fête, she runs into the bush to deliver her child, Tubman, with the assistance of her partner, Melonhead, and douen sister, Abitefa. Tan-Tan's rush to get back to Abitefa specifically in order to deliver her child challenges the narratives about animacy and medical assistance. First, it is noteworthy that Tan-Tan goes to Abitefa for comfort and assistance with obstetrics. Most medicalized narratives eschew animal presence and rely heavily on technology so much so that the birthing experience is as far away from natural childbirth as possible, avoiding even the taint (pun intended) of thinking of humans as animals. Second, Abitefa's presence (though only hinted at) complicates the relationship between humans and animals as rehabilitative. After all, Abitefa behaves like a sister: helping Tan-Tan adjust to life among the douen, resenting her presence and fighting with Tan-Tan, accompanying Tan-Tan out to forbidden places to make mischief as Robber Queen, drinking alcohol, and interfering with Tan-Tan's love life.[45] It is impossible to read Abitefa as a pet, though Melonhead makes that mistake, earning Abitefa's ire. Tan-Tan and Abitefa's relationship complicates and extends the discourses around animacy, madness and rehabilitation, namely that animal companions must be subdued and those who need them are little more than animals themselves. Again, Hopkinson worries the line between Black humans and animals. The ableist narrative that would devalue Tan-Tan's need for comfort stems from similar logics of animacy that would relegate Abitefa to existing solely in service to Tan-Tan. Instead, Hopkinson insists on a robust animal character who often does not make Tan-Tan's comfort her priority. The narrative unmakes a definition of madness that places animacy-as-abjection at the crux of ableist ideology.

Hopkinson's use of Tan-Tan and Quamina as mad Black figures calls for a set of interpretive strategies that permit their disruptive potential within the text. *Midnight Robber* is also a theoretical intervention in narrative form, since it meditates on the way mad Blackness can structure ontology (through the characters of Quamina and Tan-Tan), and epistemology of reader and character. Hopkinson uses artificial intelligence, called Granny Nanny, to structure the lives of the characters and the text. Within the novel (a specifically text based form), Granny Nanny emphasizes the aural. She disrupts the linearity seemingly required to discipline subjects into narrative. Granny Nanny also foregrounds that mad Blackness is not always benign or benevolent. I will address these in that order. The Granny Nanny interface is built upon calypso rhythms, indicating that sound creates technology differently than the eye, a direct challenge to ocular-centric technology based on African diasporic cultural paradigms. As one character describes, a programmer ran "the Nanny messages through a sound filter; tonal instead of text-based, understand? The day them was set to wipe she memory, Nanny start to sing to Marryshow ... Nannysong is only a hundred and twenty-seven tones, and she does only sing basic phrases to we; numbers and simple stock sentences and so."[46] The calypso rhythms hearken to a pan-Caribbean heritage and provide a lens through which to understand technology as aurally based rather than an issue of readerly or nonsensual mechanics. Those who are more fluent in nannysong can sing to her, and "so long as Nanny don't see no harm to life nor limb, she will lock out all but she overruling protocols for a little space."[47] Granny Nanny works through nanomites, small robots, within the soil and in the ear. As an orifice, the ear controls not only sound but depth perception and other forms of proprioception as well. To invoke the sonic is to question how one understands reality itself.[48] When we hear, we do so much more than just absorb sound. We understand our reality based on how we interpret and absorb that sound. The process, highlighted here by interaction with artificial intelligence, requires that characters and readers harness and rely on sound as a modality for interaction, an obligation punctuated in the text by the injection of onomatopoeia such as "swips!" "bup!" and "plang-palang!"

As noted above in the discussions of Quamina and Tan-Tan, speech and silence occupy a vexed position in the text. Granny Nanny's emphasis on sound shifts the emphasis on the (typically silent) visual act of reading,[49] but also, like interruptions to the ear and strange noise, acts as a destabilizing force. It is clear that the reader is supposed to be listening to an orator. The beginnings of the book ask the reader/listener to "trust me and let me distract you little bit with one anansi story."[50] The epigraph reads, "I stole the torturer's tongue." Combined, the two emphasize that the readerly experience will not be merely about words on the page but also the sonics of the text. To my mind, this is not just about the paradox of representing the voice in speech, à la Henry Louis Gates Jr.'s "talking book," but also about the disruption of the ocular as the primary interpretative lens, and about how sound, in this case Black sound, governs our understanding of speech. An emphasis on the sonic questions first how much one trusts a readerly text to convey sound, and, second, how Black sound undermines that which a readerly text has typically been asked to confirm. Since it is true that "the Nansi Web has its origin in language rather than space, this points to the novel's ultimate suggestion for a community governed by bonds of language and orality rather than body and colour."[51] Then it is also true that "Hopkinson's work is motivated by a dialectical formal logic that militantly opposes the discretionary binaries of mind/body, developed/developing, inner/outer, and so on and attempts to restore or invent a perspective capable of penetrating these perceptual barriers."[52] Yet, Hopkinson's work does more than perform a Derridean analysis of logophilia and place the Cartesian mind/body split under erasure. *Midnight Robber* refuses to sediment the idea that the aural/sonic is automatically better than the written. Considering the constellation of relationships to Tan-Tan vis-à-vis her performance at the fête and the multiple meanings of Quamina's silence, the sonic confuses just as much as the ocular and calls into question the uncritical influence of both. In short, the sonic opens up the possibilities for community, and it also opens up the possibilities for (mis)interpretation. Here, the sonic is mad Black.

Granny Nanny not only operates as an instance of mad Blackness based on her composition, but as the narrator of the tale Granny Nanny disrupts the linear progression of the story. Granny Nanny interjects itself into the narrative temporarily or permanently to provide some pause to the action. Some of the interruptions are short and ask the listener/reader to be patient. In others, the narrator privileges the middle of the story not as merely happenings toward a particular end but rather part of a lesson. The narrator interrupts to tell folktales about Tan-Tan so that the listener receives a textured understanding of the intervening events in the novel itself. I agree that "the folktales function as autonomous gaps within the totality of the novel the very existence of which both allows us to think relationally (or dialogically) and forces us to develop provisional explanations in order to assimilate these departures back into the primary narrative. In short, the folktales enable us to perceive the narrative *as narrative*, as a systemic structure of meaning-making that is always unfinished or in process."[53] In this way, Granny Nanny's interventions enact the self-referential, fragmentary pastiche and play associated with most postmodern texts. Yet, her mad Blackness is not easily collapsible as such because her disruptions seek total control over the narrative by crafting the stories and interjecting them as an act of disruptive pleasure. Simultaneously, Granny Nanny's interruptions react against the possibility of acquiring complete control since they also demonstrate the impossibility of completely accessing the characters or meanings within the confines of one linear story. Granny Nanny operates as a technology of mad Blackness, destabilizing the purchase of multiple philosophical—modern and postmodern—claims to truth and knowledge. Mad Blackness refuses linear temporality, invaginates space, deposes ocular for sonic knowledge, embraces silence, pursues control, and relinquishes power, all at the same time.

Clearly, Granny Nanny is no benign technological interface,[54] and by extension mad Blackness will not always act as such either. One critic calls attention to the fact that a nonhuman interface narrates the entire story: "Hopkinson's storytelling clearly supports the importance of narrative production, that crucial step between the database and the audience, but when that production is controlled by the machine that *is* the database, she plunges us right back into the anxiety of the missing human."[55] Of course, the critic refers here to the Granny Nanny interface itself, since it governs how the citizens of Toussaint understand their life stories. When they urinate, the interface analyzes the contents of the toilet. Even though the story relies on orality as a foundational aspect, the nonhuman storyteller has so mastered the craft of storytelling that it replaces the human storyteller and displaces human authority. This becomes troubling for a variety of reasons, not least of which is that the Granny Nanny interface upends human claims to creativity and narrative in this fashion, and undermines human agency. It is imperative to acknowledge the cry of opposition: Granny Nanny was composed by humans based on calypso rhythms and, therefore, is not much more than an advanced robot. The citizens of Toussaint (Marryshevites) willingly inject themselves with the technology given by the Marryshow Corporation, and understand Granny Nanny as a potentially benign overlord. However, Granny Nanny searches for Tan-Tan across the dimension veils, evincing an agency no one anticipated. Her interventions raise theodicy questions: What else did Granny Nanny know, if she knew Tan-Tan was pregnant with Antonio's child? And, since Granny Nanny had enough power to shift the nanomites within Tan-Tan to her unborn child, did Granny Nanny allow Tan-Tan to endure the pregnancy and all of her trauma for the end result of a progeny that could better solidify Granny Nanny's power?[56]

To my mind, the mad Blackness inherent in Granny Nanny's technological power becomes anxiogenic not solely because it disrupts a belief in the complete uniqueness of human creative autonomy and agentive production and thereby dismantles certain claims to humanity. Given the reminder that Granny Nanny is an African diasporic creation, I would point out that the anxiety is about the missing Black human and Black creative toil. In this way, Granny Nanny intensifies the presence of Blackness, being a reminder and remainder of its creative cultural power. She also questions the common definitions of Blackness that link it to specific bodies alone. Certainly, I do not suggest that Blackness is determined by what Black people produce culturally. However, I do wish to call attention to how Black cultural production has become a marker of the presence of Blackness and in some cases synonymous with Blackness itself. To my mind, Hopkinson's text envisions a useful but limited delinking of Black identity and Black creative power. In this paradigm, race broadly and Blackness in particular become "a set of articulated political relations . . . and not a biological or cultural descriptor."[57] Mad Blackness then disrupts and refigures an unquestioned heralding of creative power as a shorthand for or part of a cursory definition of the (Black) human.

In this conversation, I sought to contextualize madness in communities of Blackness rather than in exclusive relation to a white cisheteropatriarchal norm. Theorizing the concept of the mad Black or mad Blackness opens up the space to consider how the discourses of madness and Blackness not only operate in intraracial intimate spaces but also intensify and dismantle common understandings of each other. In the next conversation, I continue contemplating what it means to undo Blackness and madness. Undoing takes on a different valence. Whereas this discussion understands undoing as a moment of destabilization, the next focuses on it as a deliberate act of disengagement. In particular, I wonder: what does it mean to disengage from the categories that make madness and Blackness theoretically possible?

:: CONVERSATION 3

ABANDONING THE HUMAN?

> The Good News of their
>
> pure monkeyshine chicanery must be put away now.
> All headlines and any waiting new world phylum
>
> must never be reported or filed. Their Black boy joy,
> on this slick well-named street, must remain untelevised.
>
> I know history &
> (you know) what happens next.
>
> —NIKKY FINNEY, "Segregation, Forever," *Head Off & Split*

The ideological conceit of the human materializes at every turn. It operates as the main thrust of an argument about the (in)validity of Black and mad subjects' existence. As it becomes an appeal to or for a purported universal experience, it ironically denies some humans a humanity according to Western European ideals, which are fundamentally anti-Black and sanist. Since it masquerades as normalcy, it insidiously functions as an apparition—ghosting a text or an event. Conceptually, humanity separates the human from flora and fauna and ostensibly guarantees that a human will be thought of as an autonomous subject, operating with agency and securing the legal, social, cultural, political, and material conditions to do so. For mad Black subjects, this definition of the human does not apply.

This understanding of humanity, forged in the crucible of the Enlightenment period, undergirds our analytic praxis as well. Its materiality affects the access Black mad subjects are granted to particular conditions and, as a discursive construct, adherence to it affects the theoretical paradigms with which we work in literary criticism. This is the break where the criticism reveals itself to itself: this notion of humanity lingers in the criticism that art—exclusive to humans, of course—must have specific characteristics (formalism). As the previous conversation intimates, it subtends our attention to and preoccupation with ocularity and the logos (deconstruction, structuralism). It assumes that readers' seldom autonomous interpretations evince the value of meaning in a text (reader-oriented criticism). It occupies our concerns about interiority (psychoanalysis) and labor (Marxism) since it finds critical purchase in the energy expended by certain human bodies and minds (feminist criticism, queer studies, disability studies, ethnic studies, etc.).

Sedimented within our interpretive strategies and invested with promise—so much so since we refer to ourselves as humanists—the concept of the human becomes nearly impossible to critically examine. The ideology of the human carries with it an exclusivity: namely, that the category of human belongs solely to a figure Rosemarie Garland Thomson terms the normate. Such a figure—white, male, cis gendered, straight, able-bodied, Protestant—excludes multiple identity categories on its face.[1] Because of its origins in the Enlightenment and entanglement with the Middle Passage, eugenics, imperialism/colonialism, and the carceral system, the human poses a set of ontic and narratological problems for Black madness and mad Blackness. In the previous conversations within this text we've seen how the concept of the human could be opened up, the cut widened, when an artist-theorist places Blackness and madness at the center rather than the periphery. For instance, Butler uses Ina to theorize about the constellation of intimate relationships available when Blackness and madness form the crux of a new identity. Hopkinson's cognitively disabled and mentally ill characters shift the narratological terrain when their specific minds become the locus of the novel. Each artist-theorist questions how capacious the category of human can be. What boundaries keep humans fundamentally human? If remaining human is possible or preferable, what exactly does it mean to be one? How might we read and interpret if we cannot assume the validity of the human?

Following a politics of curiosity,[2] I conjecture about what it might mean to unmake madness and Blackness, detract from the critical and narrative power each has accrued as derogatory. Though I consider that both discourses were fomented in the Enlightenment as a way of defining and disciplining nonnormative bodies, I am not interested in turning to conversations between Enlightenment thinkers (or those wrestling within that tradition). I am much more interested in the critical gaps and folds explored by Black studies and disability studies thinkers. Their analyses invaginate our discussions, forcing us to examine how we think about madness and Blackness in a world hostile to them. This discussion comes from two strains: one, from the previous conversations in this project in which nonhuman characters populate the landscape, and, two, from a larger conversation beyond this project about the potential of madness and Blackness to be disruptive once one divests from the human as a category or concept. I turn to those in disability and Black studies who have theorized about the creation of human and humanity as a concept vis-à-vis madness and Blackness. I purpose to trace their understanding of this concept and, since the two have often implicated but not involved each other, I also aim to find the common conceptual ground between them.[3] Last, I turn to artist-theorist Tananarive Due's *African Immortals* series as a mad Black text that operates as a heuristic, questions the validity of human as a concept, and explores the repercussions of abandoning it. Though I read the text as a set of experiments, I concentrate on a few overarching story lines—desiring Blackness, understanding the ideology of ability, and forming new interpretive strategies—that question whether the conception of the human has particular narrative power.

Other F-Words: Fugitivity, Fungibility, & Futility

Scholars within Black studies have long contested the category of human for Black people. Sylvia Wynter's oeuvre contains a rigorous and adroit critique of this concept, designating the human as a localized Judeo Christian concept that she terms Man.[4] She traces it through the Enlightenment to the late twentieth-century Caribbean, citing that the human was ideologically designed to exclude Indigenous people and Blacks.[5] There could be no room for those whose subjugation made colonial and imperial life possible. To be clear, this subjugation was not simply about putting those bodies to work, and harnessing their labor, but also about the intellectual subjugation and cultural denigration of those bodies. They had to be deployed in service of the colonial and imperial subject physically, and simultaneously disregarded as a space of intellectual and cultural complexity. The prohibitions against reading, gathering, and marriage (just to name a few) ensured that the Black cultural and social institutions developed did not carry with them the validating stamp of approval from social institutions that had power. Excising Blackness from histories (read: time) makes permissible the kind of erasure that facilitates thinking of Blacks as outside the realm of the human. Moreover, the emphasis on labor sustained a set of practices that sought to create a permanent underclass from the antebellum period to the present. Blackness then not only bears the mark of being thought of as having a fundamental lack of humanity, but that lack is determined, and circumscribed, by fungibility and fugitivity. Race, then, and Blackness specifically, determines who lives and who dies.[6] As a result of this thanatological constraint, Blackness remains exteriorized, consistently unaccounted for in the construction of the modern world.[7]

Even after Man, to deploy the term in Wynter's lexicon for the human, definitions of Blackness must contend with abjection. The analytical praxis consistently turns and returns to the areas where Blackness has a circumscribed agency, limns a limited radicality, and remains enmeshed with histories of violence and degradation. Scholars differ on their responses to abjection such that some attempt to maneuver out of it, and others accept it as part of the experiences of Blackness. To be clear, accepting abjection is not equivalent to accepting institutionalized racism. Instead, it requires viewing Black social life as lived in light of social death,[8] or finding freedom in unfreedom. Jared Y. Sexton's notion that Blacks live in light of social death dovetails with Fred Moten's understanding of freedom in unfreedom in one crucial way: that abjection must be circumnavigated if one exists. The difference between the two scholars' arguments resides in how that navigation takes place and with what affective residues. That is, radicality and resistance evince an ontology circumscribed by the discourses of fugitivity and fungibility. Locating the origins of these discourses in the antebellum period, some scholars also find that abjection must be understood as a fundamental aspect of Black life post–Middle Passage. These scholars— among them Kimberly Juanita Brown, Saidiya Hartman, Christina Sharpe, Hortense Spillers, and Alexander Weheliye—all understand the long reach of the antebellum period as having direct repercussions to how Black life functions currently. Slavery as a vast hemispheric project fundamentally shapes how Blacknesses operate discursively and materially.[9] The residues of unspoken, ethical grammars force those who find some degree of maneuverability possible to wrestle with some exigencies, such as the queered and erotic Black/white encounter or the presumed degradation of male rape as a locus of Black radical power.[10] Man tethers itself to Blackness through abjection, requiring Blackness to make meaning through a grammar that enfolds within it the resistance to itself. Abjection becomes the facet of Blackness (not Blackness in toto) typified by the fact that "you can't win. You can't break even. And, you can't get out of the game."[11]

Whereas the field of Black studies has chosen to question the validity of the human as a concept, disability studies has taken a decidedly different strategy. Disability studies makes a particular claim on the human even as it acknowledges that the category excludes disability as a matter of course. For instance, myriad scholars clarify that the conception of health and ability determines who is included and who is worthy of living. Lives thought to be too painful, deformed, or requiring too much medical intervention often fight for the right to live at all.[12] The typical disability studies response has been to depict disability as a part of human variance, a part of the spectrum of human experience. This particular formulation correlates to the idea that if one lives long enough, one will become disabled. The kingdom of the sick, as Sontag puts it, always welcomes new visitors and permanent residents.[13] Undergirding this idea is the conception of the human as potentially inclusive of disability, where disability can function as an absent presence. According to disability studies scholars, this absent presence surfaces in narrative, art, and rhetoric, among other cultural and social spaces. For instance, the Venus de Milo makes its current claim to beauty based on its amputee status.[14] In *Keywords for Disability Studies*, the entry on aesthetics positions disability as hopeful prospect despite its position and history: "The close proximity of aesthetic judgment to carceral isolation and rationalized euthanasia is the darker side of Enlightenment knowledge, even as the increased visibility of the disabled body creates the occasion for its liberation."[15] Narrative relies on intellectual disability even when it is not named as such or embodied within a character.[16] Communication requires the disabled body to establish itself not only as coherent but also saleable in terms of diversity.[17] In each of these instances, the human is a category to which disabled people already belong, albeit in abjected and absented form. The idea is not only that the human relies on disability to perform conceptual work but also that enfolded into the human is the experience of disability.

Tobin Siebers makes this point most forcefully when describing the "ideology of ability": a formulation to which we are all in thrall since it determines how we consider our futures, pasts, presents, and selves.[18] The ideology of ability, according to him, determines how we understand identity itself because we are all wedded to a desire to be healthy or well or able. The only way to excise ourselves from this ideology—were such a thing possible—would be to reconceptualize disability, or in the words of Robert McRuer "come to desire it."[19] I find Siebers's concept useful in so far as it describes a modality that governs our imaginations about disability specifically and the human writ large. In thinking of its relationship to the human, the ideology of ability shuttles us away from the capaciousness of the category human. According to Siebers, the ideology of ability shuts down conversations and imaginative possibilities, theories and experiences of embodiment that are germane to the human but foreclosed based on said ideological construct. In this way, disability studies embraces a curious rhetorical move, positioning disability as "too high to get over, Too low to get under."[20] Though disability is excluded from the human, the field depicts this as an oversight, a powerful one, but one that can be rectified by thinking of and incorporating disability as universal. In part, this explains why so many disability studies projects justify themselves by claiming disability as a base identity or rhetoric: "Disability is the other other that makes otherness possible."[21] "It is the master trope of disqualification."[22] Within these formulations, disability is not only what determines the human but its better inclusion will also define the category of human so that it can begin to include everyone.

Both strategies for engaging the human have merit: find the traces of what and who is used to constitute the concept and underscore the processes by which the human creates itself as superior. Recall that the mad Black is both an embodied positionality and an aesthetic intervention. As such, it hints at some common conceptual ground and useful disagreements. The mad Black cannot so simply slip into history as an aberration, nor can it so easily slip out of history as a failure. Here, the mad Black advocates a consistent questioning of how abjection functions, and from where it arises. It also acts as an adroit poker player. It sees the ideology of ability and raises it the possessive investment in whiteness (*pace* George Lipsitz), questioning how one arrives at universality if the so-called soundness of the bodymind is not the sole reason for exclusion. That is, the mad Black reveals a set of breaks to read: without a reliance on ocularity and a skepticism about linear conceptions of time and narrative, it disrupts the easy alignment of disability with whiteness or Blackness with degradation. Reading these breaks requires the disruption courted by Sylvia Wynter's refusal of the category Man and broaches what Siebers termed the "conceptual horizon" marked by the ideology of ability.[23] Mad Blackness calls for no less than a retooling of the terms of humanity itself. It questions the desire for ability, and the desire for whiteness. Since the Enlightenment positions madness and Blackness as a set of "ontological foils for the modern, rational, European subject,"[24] the fissures reveal where, how, and with whom current ideological investments lie. Further, their undoing and unmaking requires an unmooring that reckons with constructs that have heretofore been unavailable.

As my previous comments suggest, there exist a few cultural and social locations that allow us to question the utility of the human. Specifically, the appeal to universality and the possessive investment in whiteness cohere in one's relationship to the nation-state. How is one defined as a citizen if madness or Blackness functions as a default disqualification? Those scholars working on physical disability have given a cursory nod to abjection,[25] madness forces disability studies to reckon with where abjection arises and how it might be embraced.[26] Taking a methodological cue from Nirmala Erevelles, who explores what it might mean to embrace disability as a part of Blackness, we need to examine abjection as a social location where Blackness and madness can powerfully defang the critical purchase of the human. It is not coincidental that much of the work on madness comes from the fields of rhetoric and composition because so many of the narratives we embrace about madness view it as a fundamental issue of communication. These scholars intervene in the sacralized understanding of madness as uncommunicative and therefore unripe for analysis in perpetuity. Madness and Blackness exert hortatory pressure on all modes of critical analysis, forcing an examination of how we place the human at the center or overlook it as the default premise.[27]

Mad Black Human Trials

Since reconceptualizing the human requires that we rethink at least the relationship to the nation-state, the role of abjection, and our modes of analysis, I turn to an artist-theorist that provides an apt heuristic for doing so. Tananarive Due's *African Immortals* series (1997–2011) follows the lives of several newly made immortals and other (older) immortals as they sort through the demarcations of humanity and its repercussions for them and their power. Like Nalo Hopkinson's text, Due's work operates primarily within a Black cultural context in which madness is a fundamental aspect of the narrative landscape and the characters' experience. In its entirety, the series is mad Black: it disrupts the linearity of Western history and conceptions of time, and it complicates the reliance on ocularity to determine meaning. Keep in mind that madness operates as both psychosocial and biopsychiatric (and this critical conversation is skeptical of both paradigms). Madness in this series takes the forms of material reality and metaphor. First, the characters experience a racialized paranoia based on the panoptic structure of their lives. The paranoia does not merely exist as a feature of the characters' experience; it surfaces as part of the aesthetic architecture of the series itself, in its premises and narrative structure. In fact, the characters' paranoia propels the series as a heuristic endeavor, experimenting with how their anxiety about who/what they are reveals the limitations of and possibilities for being human and for human beings. Second, a character who becomes the protagonist of the third and fourth installments would be considered mentally ill in her world since she experiences cognitive symptoms that mark her as neuroatypical. The series becomes a heuristic that crystallizes the notion that the abandonment of the human is an experimentation in ideology, a desire to tap into the possibility of a different kind of world. My analysis does not push toward a resolution (i.e., whether one should or can leave the human behind), but rather reads how Due's text experiments with the problems created by the human and all that it entails with whiteness, maleness, and ability at its center. In what follows, I examine three questions that arise within Due's experiment and test the category of the human: what it means to desire Blackness; how the ideology of ability surfaces; and what interpretive strategies result when we seek to abandon the human.

First, a summary: Each of the four novels opens up a conversation about what is fundamental to humanity. In testing why, how, and, ultimately, if the category human has purchase for Blacks across the diaspora, the human characters and those recently human (now immortal) must wrestle with their habits from, obligations to, and affinity for human life. The first novel, *My Soul to Keep* (1997), tests what it means to desire Black life forever.[28] It follows one of fifty-nine life brothers, David/Dawit Wolde, who has been given immortality by his so-called father, Khaldun, who stole the blood of Christ. David breaks both of the prohibitions regarding the blood: don't tell and don't share. Initially, to keep his secret, he murders his child from his previous family in 1920s Black Chicago and his wife's uncle who recognizes him from the same time period. The novel culminates in his desire to share the blood with his wife, Jessica, and their five-year-old daughter. Though he successfully makes his wife an immortal, he kills his five-year-old daughter in the process. *The Living Blood* (2001) follows the newly made immortal, Jessica, and her now toddler daughter who was made immortal in the womb, Fana.

Fana's discovery of her powers—including mind reading and telekinesis—results in a category five hurricane and their being hunted by the son of another life brother who has used his father's blood to stay alive for two centuries. This novel questions the function and repercussions of the ideology of ability, asking what gets sacrificed in the desire for wellness and longevity.

The third novel, *Blood Colony* (2008), attempts to discern what if anything can be gained when Blackness and madness operate outside the confines of the nation-state. Fana, now a teenager, distributes her healing blood across the globe, drawing the attention of another immortal-born, Charlie/Michel. Charlie/Michel and his father, Stefan, belong to another sect, Sanctus Cruor (comprised of Italian immortals and some acolytes hoping for immortality), who believe that the Earth needs to be cleansed of heretics and sinners. Such a cleansing would occur after Charlie/Michel marries his prophesied mate, whom Sanctus Cruor believes to be Fana. Charlie/Michel mentally manipulates the African immortals to kidnap Jessica, Fana, and their family and bring them to Mexico for the nuptials he attempts to force between himself and Fana. In an exertion of will, Fana refuses to join him because he has tricked her and she is opposed to his idea of a cleansing, citing (among other objections) that he draws his power from an evil source, the shadows, whereas she prefers a more moral plane. The final novel in the series, *My Soul to Take* (2011), questions what analyses we require to move outside of the repercussions caused by an investment in the human. In this novel, Charlie/Michel begins the cleansing and Fana tries to stop him as he uses his considerable power to mentally manipulate her and those around her.

Madness surfaces within this series in the same ways that it appears in Butler's or Hopkinson's work: aesthetic and embodied. It is a mad Black text. With regard to the embodied experience of one or more characters, there are characters who are driven out of their minds by the mental manipulation and telekinetic control of other characters. Fana's superlative telekinetic abilities, because they are uncontrolled and untrained, tend to function as a set of cognitive disabilities and her anxiety about them, as mental illness. Also, madness becomes part of the aesthetic enterprise of the novel, demonstrating that, as Michael Bérubé affirms, "disability and ideas about disability can be and have been put to use in fictional narratives in ways that go far beyond any specific rendering of any disabled character or characters."[29] Due's *African Immortals* series engages ideas about disability, particularly madness, as part of the structure of the text. For instance, the base rule of this world is not only that immortals exist but also that they are a group of Black men who (as we find out in the third book) have been hunted since the colonial period for their blood. The very framework of the series draws on the interrelated discourses of Blackness and paranoia. *African Immortals* is careful not to suggest a causal link between Blackness and paranoia, but Due's work does question the construction of Blackness-as-abject in which paranoia becomes a useful lens through which to approach the world. Paranoia as madness harkens to biopsychiatric definitions about which I am skeptical; however, as a part of a Black episteme, it could speak to a mad Black orientation developed toward an anti-Black sanist world.

This orientation allows paranoia to form an overarching penumbral presence for the premise of the novel. Specifically, the idea of African immortals dovetails with the beliefs of Five Percenters or the Nation of Gods and Earths, a faith founded by a former member of the Nation of Islam. It teaches not only that Black men are gods but also that there is a conspiracy to keep that fact quiet. John Jackson explicitly links this belief system to what he terms racial paranoia in his monograph of the same name. Jackson understands the Five Percenters as a reaction to what he terms *de cardio* racism, the racism that remains unspoken as remnants of slavery and Jim Crow systems and ideology. Five Percenters' beliefs, Jackson claims, align with the idea that Western governments and multinational corporations conspire against Black people to keep them disenfranchised and marginalized. The African immortal men in this series realize the central idea to Five Percenter beliefs: Black men are preyed upon for the deity within. The idea that their blood is stolen from Christ explicitly links these men to the divine, and implies that they themselves are deities on earth. Even though they do not make themselves out to be gods, their power over some people's lives or deaths provides them with a consummate power. There are significant differences between the Five Percenter beliefs and Due's text, most important of which is that not all African and African-descendant men are immortal. Yet, every time the life brothers have to face discrimination in the world or have to blend in based on their Blackness, this idea lurks at the surface. Such is the case with paranoia as it interacts with the text: the truth is slippery and remains unintelligible because it is never clear. Paranoia tows the line between being a biopsychiatric symptom and Black epistemology.

The *African Immortals* series tests the category of the human through all four novels. There are perhaps more experiments within Due's series, but I consider three major concerns: how or whether the human has purchase when one desires Blackness (forever); how the ideology of ability functions;

and, finally, what happens if/when the modes of analysis that privilege the human fall apart for those it was designed to protect. Due's heuristic does not neatly start and end with each novel, so I offer a set of analyses that move across the novels through the story lines. My aim is to pinpoint how Due has questioned the human and the uneasy solutions offered in the world she crafts.

Beginning with *My Soul to Keep*, Due's work suggests that a desire for Blackness in perpetuity upends one of the main thrusts of the human. Being Black forever is a mighty long time. She creates an immortal character through whom we read multiple eras in history, David/Dawit Wolde. His experiences with colonialism and slavery inform the framework through which we understand humanity. It is not merely that his immortality must be understood through his Blackness but that the notion of humanity should be understood within the context of anti-Blackness. That is, as the Black studies scholars above have intimated, there is no conception of humanity that is not already mired in anti-Blackness. David/Dawit fought against the Italians during the Battle of Adwa and, later, became a slave. He refused to be a breeder, decided to run away, and was lynched. (Please note here the impossibility of the grammatical parallel because David/Dawit cannot claim agency over his own murder.) David/Dawit also chooses to create two families, one in the height of segregation during the 1920s Jazz Age in Chicago, and his final family in the early twenty-first century in Florida. Each time he chooses Black women as partners, and during the Jazz Age he explicitly participated in African American cultural traditions. He later capitalizes on those cultural traditions by writing a book about the Jazz Age, thereby inserting himself in a tradition of Black intellectualism. The series aligns immortality with Blackness (at least at first) and the cruelty of mortals with anti-Blackness.

The later novels reveal that the desire for Blackness—either in immortal or mortal form—collides with foundational institutional structures. Even when the Black characters are human, they experience the historical entrenchment of racism and Jim Crow either in their family experience or as a continuous pressure with which they must live. When they are immortal, their immortality becomes a prophylaxis against the literal murder of Black bodies in an anti-Black world, but it cannot staunch the encroachment of structures such as colonialism, slavery, Jim Crow, and the prison industrial complex that take for granted the inhumanity of Black people the world over. For instance, the life brothers choose to sequester themselves in Lalibela, Ethiopia, desiring to remain outside the clutches of the nation-state. This proves difficult to sustain for a host of practical reasons—interface with the public being one of them. The other issue is ideological. To desire Blackness is to wrestle with what history has wrought in terms of anti-Blackness. David's choice to be a jazz musician evinces some commitment to experiencing and creating out of the degradation of Jim Crow. Channeling the caution of Stuart Hall, Black (Canadian) studies scholar Rinaldo Walcott reminds us that the production of Black popular culture exists within the tensions of belonging and not-quite-citizen, even as the nation-state exerts pressure on its Black occupants to adhere to narratives about multiculturalism and national belonging.[30] So, David/Dawit's immersion in jazz indexes a desire for a specific kind of Blackness: one that avowedly celebrates Black cultural forms, unapologetically so.

In *Blood Colony*, the immortals' involvement in the Battle of Adwa surfaces as another mode through which David/Dawit and his brothers attempt to desire Blackness, and avoid the power of an anti-Black nation-state. David/Dawit and his brothers undertake a special parallel mission during the Battle of Adwa, under the guise of counseling Emperors Taytu and Menelik, to triumph over the Italian soldiers searching for the Lalibela colony and, with it, the secrets of the immortal blood. Due's invocation of Adwa, the Ethiopians' real-life victory over Italy's colonialist effort, signals a narratological desire for Black independence, since this military victory calls attention to itself as a decisive rebuttal to anti-Blackness and colonial rule. Though historian Raymond Jonas introduces the Battle of Adwa as an exception (with all that intimates regarding it as fluke or coincidence), the rest of his historical study delineates the shrewd calculations on the part of Menelik, Taytu, and other Ethiopians that set them up for victory at Adwa.[31] The events of the late nineteenth century shadow Due's fictional texts such that Black defiance, military might, and resistance color the interactions with the Italian immortals. Stefan, the only member of Sanctus Cruor David/Dawit and the life brothers left alive, remains bitter after a century. Any mention of Adwa makes his jaw clench.[32] Through David/Dawit's choices in the United States and in Ethiopia, Due's text invokes the anti-Black nation-state to press on the desire for and defense of Blackness in a world hostile to it, thereby challenging Blackness-as-abject in the category of the human. David/Dawit can avoid succumbing to these pressures in part because of his immortality: he cannot die and he does not have to invest in whiteness for survival of any sort.

Yet, if his immortality is the pragmatic solution within the world of the novels, the ideological one rests in Due's recourse to memory. Drawing on Toni Morrison's conception of "rememory" as a collective endeavor, I would argue that Dawit/David's story line opens up the possibility for anamnesis, which is at base reminiscence. Here, I consider the lay definition of anamnesis, a recollection, but also the Platonic ideal of recuperating past knowledge through reason. Reading Anne Donadey read Octavia E. Butler's *Kindred*, Donadey points out that postcolonial and US ethnic narratives suffuse their understanding of the Platonic ideal with the collective. Rather than secure knowledge that is unitary and singular, she avers, these narratives position anamnesis as a process that "is collective rather than individual and always yields fragmentary rather than complete knowledge."[33] Anamnesis allows for the gaps that mad Black texts create: the process uncomfortably rests with collective, fragmentary knowledge and memory as an incomplete solution to supposedly official anti-Black histories and, more generally speaking, the presumption of abjection. In addition to being a process that emphasizes collectivity (a different kind of reason from the individuality championed by Enlightenment ideals), anamnesis in the *African Immortals* series also invokes the medical definitions of the term: medical history of a patient and quickened immunological responses to pathogens to which one has already been exposed. Thinking of this kind of memory as an immunological response suggests protection, hinting at memory in the same way as Fred Moten or Sylvia Wynter. The breaks. The gaps. The fissures. These open up the possibility of viewing Due's created and recuperated histories through David/Dawit as part of a systematic response to anti-Blackness. In that way, David/Dawit's narrative—participating/coercing the Battle of Adwa, resisting slavers' demand that he rape, choosing Black families, becoming a jazz musician, and writing himself into a Black studies tradition—reconfigures history such that Blackness can be loved, desired, and hoped for even as it resists the abjection wrought by anti-Black world-making.

Within Due's heuristic, another question surfaces alongside whether one can desire Blackness: namely, whether one should desire ability. That is, how does the ideology of ability surface? Frankly, a series about immortal healing blood by default raises questions about the ideology of ability and the attraction to being able-bodied. (These questions are also enmeshed in discussions about race, since racialization processes are based on notions about blood.[34]) Here, Due's work tests how much the investment in ability costs, even when adherence to it proves dangerous or foolhardy. Keep in mind that the ideology of ability delimits the imagination about the future, but remains toothsome because able-bodiedness seems to offer a life without physical or mental limits. In *The Living Blood*, Jessica and Fana are chased by a two-hundred-year-old son of one of the life brothers, who acquired his father's blood by exsanguinating him repeatedly. After having amassed significant wealth, the son chooses to acquire more immortal blood at all costs: willing his employees to rape, murder, and torture. The blood does not provide this villain with what he desires, since he bemoans his life as a wheelchair user, complaining to his father that he has been "reduced to this."[35] The deictic phrase leaves the disability unnamed, mobilizing an ableist grammar for the unspeakable fate into which the son has been supposedly forced because of his father's negligence and lack of love. Due's text suggests that other characters harbor an unquestioned desire for ability, affectively linking disability with disgust. Notably, Dawit/David's interiority depicts this most vividly: "[He] sucked in a breath when he saw the small wrinkled man . . . hideous, a creature whose appearance offended him so deeply that, for a moment, Dawit felt a visceral fright. He'd often witnessed mortals' deformity with age, but he had never fathomed that nature could produce such a shrunken ruined oddity."[36] David/Dawit's meditations and the son's comment reveal the obdurate desire for able-bodiedness. Yet, lurking within David/Dawit's reaction and the son's pleading for the blood is the casuistry of desiring ability, since it is imbricated with so many other desires. Both David/Dawit and the son (hero and villain, if you will) believe ability to be the bulwark against certain forms of pain. Yet, this desire has already cost David/Dawit multiple children, and his wife, and cost this two hundred-year-old man, his father. *The Living Blood* insinuates that the cost of desiring ability may be that which ability is supposed to protect. The ideology of ability has no purchase by itself. It acquires critical heft because it appears to facilitate other prized experiences.

The preference for able-bodiedness and mental acuity actually pervades the world of the series. Due depicts a rapidly globalizing world that requires better health care in developing countries. (Her ecological and health care critiques are fairly transparent, and she makes them very clear in the acknowledgments to *Blood Colony*.) For the purposes of this discussion, I am interested in the way Due's depiction of health care drives her test of the category of human vis-à-vis the ideology of ability. In her characters' (particularly Fana's) desire to distribute their healing blood, one of the main questions before them is how to understand those who receive it. In some ways, their blood mission assumes a preference for able-bodiedness because it attempts to cure people of their ailments. Since the immortals who distribute the blood choose developing countries and low-income people, they indicate a desire to equalize access to treatment alongside a desire for ability. In this story line lies a slippage between the preference for ability and the desire for health. Due's text attempts to differentiate health disparities from the desire for superlative mental or physical ability. The former is structural and the latter, individual, so the refusal to disambiguate them agnizes how much the two discourses rely on each other for critical purchase.

Thinking of Siebers's model as a point of departure, bear in mind that he bases his understanding of the ideology of ability on disability as an identity category. Yet, as Nirmala Erevelles has demonstrated, disability cannot be embraced wholesale as an identity category when it is created in conditions facilitated by war and capitalism. Given the other story lines at stake, the text suggests the same as Erevelles: Blackness and madness as identity categories cannot be celebrated without reservation because they are not apolitical. Since they are sometimes created within oppressive conditions, the text considers the peculiar role that an ideology of ability can occupy. What happens when the preferences for able-bodiedness and able-mindedness collapse into a preference for access to wellness? The conclusion appears to be that it is not the preference for ability that excludes but rather the conditions that facilitate abjection. Humanity then has purchase in so far as Fana and others who distribute the blood desire to honor humanity in places where it has been denied. There is a question that Due's text approaches asymptotically: when Blackness and access to care no longer determine life or death, what of the ideology of ability then? What of the human then? *African Immortals* leaves open this gap, suggesting that the category of the human—when not wedded to individualism—is not driven by the same ideological conceits present in the Enlightenment version. As a result, the preference for ability might shift if community were at the crux of the category human.

Due's formal choice, placing Fana at the center of the narrative, shifts the terrain of her heuristic. Within *Blood Colony* and *My Soul to Take*, Fana reorients the understanding of ability, abjection, and the human. Her madness surfaces as a form of mental illness and cognitive difference. Because of her intense but untrained telekinetic and mind control abilities, she gets headaches and dizzy spells when she is around more than a few people. She has also been sequestered in the woods since she caused a category five hurricane at the age of three. In this way, her confinement dovetails with one of the aspects of disability that creates and sustains abjection: "Eating and living in private—due to physical and stigmatizing barriers—has defined what it has meant to be disabled. Being disabled *and* public can change what it means to be disabled and, at the same time, change the dynamics of the public—as a physical and political space."[37] When Fana goes out in public and when she escapes the compound, she upturns how madness makes meaning in the novel. It is no longer a private matter within her family that can be gently ignored; out in the world, everyone must reckon with her abilities and disabilities. They not only have to contend with the repercussions of her abilities, as she breaks into others' minds. The interaction between Fana and the outside world suggest a set of priorities regarding how her disability ought be understood. Whether she feels it as abjection or triumph raises questions about the ideological terrain of madness. Moreover, centralizing Fana as the narrative locus also radically changes which epistemologies are valid. As a disabled Black woman, a mad Black woman, her understanding of the value of personhood will be vastly different from others', especially since she has had limited experience in an anti-Black world.

When she engages in her own blood mission without her parents' consent (distributing her blood in the United States), Fana embraces Blackness, abjection, and madness. Fana operates as a mad Black character based on Due's aesthetic and content choices: she operates within the mental panopticon created by other immortals and she begins to accept and exceptionalize her headaches and dizzy spells. Buttressing her kinship with another disabled Black woman, Due fashions Fana as a twenty-first-century Harriet Tubman, citing that the apocryphal "if you're tired, keep going" "captured Tubman's spirit."[38] It is worth noting that, in the narration, others describe her as such as well, including her mother and her friend.[39] She explicitly forges kinship with people based on their relationship to the underground railroad, her modern interpretation of the antebellum network designed to bring healing blood to people within the United States. Her alignment with the disabled is not merely based on her desire to heal; it is a fundamental epistemological stance oriented toward Blackness, womanhood, and disability. As Christopher M. Bell reminds us, Harriet Tubman had a head injury that caused her to have dizzy spells, a condition that placed her in considerable danger while she worked to bring people to freedom.[40] Fana's identification invokes as much about Tubman's vocation as it does her ability status. The similarities concretize when Fana has dizzy spells because people's thoughts overwhelm her telepathic abilities. What I wish to highlight is how Fana's kinship with Harriet Tubman as a disabled Black woman aligns her with the communities she heals. Rather than the empathy described by Saidiya Hartman in which "by virtue of [one's] substitution the object of identification threatens to disappear,"[41] Fana's empathy stems from her own identification as someone who experiences stigma and danger because of her cognition and physicality. Without discounting the medicalized nature of Fana's intervention (focused mostly on cure), Fana chooses community rather than isolation and prefers to position herself as one of many rather than a singular leader. In other words, she not only identifies as disabled and abject but also identifies with the disabled and abject, forging kinship and community. Her understanding of herself and her relationship to others—including the value of their personhood—contrasts most of the foundational aspects of the human: committing to individualism, eschewing abjection, devaluing Blackness, preferring ability.

The *African Immortals* series calls into question why the white- and ability-driven concept of the human remains at the center of our analytical praxis especially since it proves so destructive for so many. George Lipsitz describes the possessive investment in whiteness primarily in economic and legal terms, but embedded in his analysis are close reading strategies that privilege antiracist commitments and politics. Taking his text to a logical conclusion, I make explicit that the possessive investment here is not just in whiteness but also in ability, and our interpretative strategies belie a commitment thereto. Within Due's series, the differentiation between health care disparities and the ideology of ability bespeaks a commitment to antiracism, given who the health disparities effect. Yet, this slippage does not constitute a wholesale rejection of the ideology of ability: the series wrestles with what interpretive strategies can do in the face of a white- and ability-driven conception of the human. For example, the preference for ability, desire for whiteness, and fear of abjection cohere in Charlie/Michel and Stefan's decision to perform a cleansing of heretics and sinners. Over the course of the last two novels, Charlie/Michel attempts to force Fana to marry him. He also begins his cleansing during their engagement, but only starts it in developing countries and impoverished areas, specifically Africa and Latin America. Charlie/Michel assumes that the power to perform the cleansing and to rule the world has been prophesied by the life brothers' father, Khaldun, in a holy document called "The Letter of the Witness." In contrast to Fana's communal ethos, Charlie/Michel rules by fiat and calls himself "the Most High." Fana not only challenges his right to rule but also his interpretation of the "Letter of the Witness." In so doing, she alters the power structure: Charlie/Michel is no longer the locus of power; they must both govern equitably. Fana also contests his limited notions of humanity and worth; his interpretative strategies no longer have the same critical purchase.

As the center of the last two novels in the series, Fana's presence and telepathy not only mark her as powerful but also challenge the certitude of Charlie/Michel's power. This shift becomes especially important because the balance of power in the novels seems to indicate which of the two the heuristic endorses as correct in their interpretations and decision making. Their births provide some useful background to understanding why the balance of power matters. Charlie/Michel is born to an Ethiopian woman and Stefan, both of whom are immortal. Khaldun (the supposed father of all the life brothers) seems to have known about him but does not alert the life brothers to his presence. Fana is born to Dawit/David and Jessica. David's transgression of the two rules about the blood—don't tell and don't share—is broadcast among the life brothers, with some being more enthusiastic about the new additions to their world than others. Khaldun's "Letter of the Witness," written two thousand years before the events of the novel, foretells the power Fana and Charlie/Michel will have together as "bringers of the blood." What isn't clear from the letter is how they will use that power or whether that power is equal.

As Fana grows into her power, she questions Charlie/Michel's supposed birthright (and hers too). Her interpretive strategies foreground how their power differential functions. If Charlie/Michel has a thirty-year head start on using his power and reading the "Letter of the Witness," what does it mean that he misinterprets the prophecy? What are the implications of his misinterpretation for analysis more broadly? Fana's challenges to him suggest not only that he profoundly misunderstands the letter but also that his approach to analyzing the world he inhabits is bankrupt, reliant as it is on white- and ability-driven notions of the human. Fana settles on consistent doubt as a useful position from which to approach all knowledge. She resides in the break or the fold in order to mount a critique. What others would label paranoia, uncertainty, and/or madness, she embraces as a fraught but fruitful epistemological position. Her presence and her interpretative posture shift the understanding of their births. First, Khaldun's attention to Fana positions her as the center of the book, upending the idea that Charlie/Michel was chosen. Khaldun's involvement in the creation of both Fana and Charlie/Michel prompts theodicy questions regarding how and why their births and powers are important for Khaldun. It is clear that Khaldun wrote the "Letter of the Witness" that forecasts their births. Less clear is why Khaldun chose to be more involved with Fana's life than with Charlie/Michel's, though the suspicion is that she is more powerful. The text intimates that Khaldun permitted both births by not telling the Lalibela colony about Charlie/Michel and explicitly warning them away from harming Fana. What seems to be an endorsement of Fana hinges on the circumstances of her birth in terms of race, and, perhaps, her gender identity. In light of his disappearance in the second installment of the *African Immortals* series, Khaldun's legacy or desires vis-à-vis Fana and Charlie/Michel remain vague though the intimation is clear: Fana, the Black girl-child reared with a Black episteme, is favored over Charlie/Michel, the mixed race boy-child reared with a colonialist and imperialist episteme.

Fana's ideological allegiance to Blackness (that is, her desire for it) redirects Charlie/Michel's plans and undoes his colonialist impulses. She was reared in a home that prized Black life: this education did not merely come through her father. It was matrilineal in that her grandmother, aunt, and mother teach her about African American history, and situate themselves geopolitically and physically (even if temporarily) in South Africa and Ethiopia. Charlie/Michel, on the other hand, was raised by his colonialist Italian father, Stefan, who participated in the anti-Black military incursion into Ethiopia. Charlie/Michel's Ethiopian mother was kept in a comatose mental state by his father; Stefan manipulates her mind so that she can perform only the simplest of tasks. Charlie/Michel demonstrates no knowledge of or interest in other parts of the world other than to control or conquer them. He and Stefan concern themselves with the acquisition of power. Fana's knowledge and validation of Black life forces her to question the underlying assumptions inherent in Charlie/Michel's interpretation of the letter. She reasons with Charlie/Michel about the "Letter of the Witness," reading it contrapuntally to point out that "the Letter never mentions killing anyone."[42] When she asks, "how did the revelation come to you, Michel? . . . Was it . . . your father's doctrine? . . . Was the Cleansing the reason he broke your mother's mind and stole you?,"[43] Fana resituates Charlie/Michel's knowledge from being objectively reasoned to being subjectively compelled by embodied urges, namely kinship with his father, a warmonger and arms dealer. Her reading of the letter also allows her to read Charlie/Michel, a tactic deploying postcolonialist and queer interpretive strategy.

Fana's read of Charlie/Michel is also an implicit read of his father, Stefan.

To be clear, I intend "read" as both interpretive strategy and queer art of insult.[44] As a figure, Stefan foregrounds the long historical and geographic reach of colonialism. He amasses power to go to war in the late nineteenth century and, though that venture fails, he continues to build his power base through the Catholic Church and several Western governments. Given that Stefan's power (and by extension Charlie/Michel's) is steeped in colonialism, the Battle of Adwa (which connects Stefan to David/Dawit and, by extension, Charlie/Michel to Fana) stands as a challenge to the infallibility and intractability of white supremacy. Historically speaking, the Battle of Adwa distinguishes itself as a victory against Italian incursion (metonymic for general European conquest) into Ethiopia (metonymic for Africa). In terms of Due's novels, this battle also marks one of the times that David/Dawit has bested (usually killed) Stefan, a feat he repeats at least once. Despite the consistent reframing of these characters as joined or separated by blood, the text cannot shake the shadow of history (both the larger historical context and the interpersonal history between Stefan and David/Dawit), a fact that Fana's read makes clear. The narration attempts to reroute this history around Charlie/Michel by describing Charlie/Michel as Latino or vaguely from the Mediterranean with copper skin and dark hair. The nods to his appearance and mixed race identity do not shake the darling buds of his white masculine privilege. By any other name, his analysis of the letter still concretizes his preferences for and commitment to a human that must be at least white and able-bodied to be valuable.[45]

When Fana reorients Charlie/Michel's reading of the letter, she exposes the faulty premises and racist, sanist whimsy within his strategies of interpretation. She forces him to articulate the reasons for his conclusions. His analysis presumes that those worth saving adhere to his understanding of morality and the human, which would not necessarily include Fana or even his mother. Certainly, the cleansing spares Stefan only because of Charlie/Michel. Charlie/Michel makes endless exceptions based on his own predilections: for instance, he kills a lover because he grows tired of her outspokenness.[46] His caprice mirrors how the boundaries of the human work. Whoever offers allegiance to the ideology represented by the human can occupy the category, even if temporarily. When Fana points out that Charlie/Michel's interpretations stem from his fealty to his father and their ideological impulses, she gives the lie to all of Charlie/Michel's analyses that stem from that premise. Fana's methodology, on the other hand, remains consistent and consistently desirous of Blackness, since she approaches her analysis with the same impulses that provoke her to model herself after Harriet Tubman. She remains acutely aware of her own abjection (and that of others) and suspicious of the linear narrative Charlie/Michel attempts to create. Her intersectional identity is not solely an embodied reality from which she develops an episteme. It becomes a set of political commitments—to Blackness and to madness—that reorient the terms of analysis themselves.

Tananarive Due ends the *African Immortals* series with an altered cleansing, one that keeps the global population healthy but also creates large amounts of infertility. This compromise between Fana and Charlie/Michel participates in the ideology of ability wholesale, since there is no longer a slippage between the need for better health care and the preference for ability. Due's aesthetic choice to resolve the narrative in this way could be read as a failure within the heuristic: specifically, that abjection and ideology of ability cannot be disappeared. Within the world of the series, the category of human maintains critical purchase for most, even with all that it excludes. Leaving these ideologies intact and functional not only reveals how much they have been absorbed into the world's systems but also how the characters' resistance to them requires communal effort and institutional dismantling. Due's narrative experiment does not offer solutions. It offers another hypothesis.

We might need a mad Black world.

:: CONVERSATION 4

NOT MAKING MEANING,
NOT MAKING SINCE (THE END THE TIME)

there's nothing delicate here. delicate
things do not survive. they get beaten up/raped/shot/
runover/knifed/poisoned or pushed into suicide
they harden, become brittle, or bend
baked under sun of years, adobe will not
yield to crop, but brick to build—
where the farmer fails, the architect prospers: a city

—WANDA COLEMAN, "Flight of the California Condor," *Imagoes*

As an inroad to an ending, I turn to the issue of whether Black madness and mad Blackness must have meaning and what that meaning must be. I disambiguate meaning and value. The former is how a concept makes sense in or has an impact on public or private space. The latter concerns an affective and sociocultural conception of relative merit or perceived worth in public or private space. In the introduction to this volume, I called this line of inquiry an act of literary theorist blasphemy because it upturns one of the basic assumptions of literary criticism: namely, that certain concepts must continue to be impactful or that those concepts must make sense in a text, that they are available to be read and understood. Yet, this kind of inquiry has a long history in Black studies and disability studies. Scholarly interventions regarding Blackness and madness call into question the utility of both meaning and value. That is, disability studies and critical race studies attend to the ways that devaluation of Blackness and madness—legally, socially, culturally, historically—contribute to the thinking of these identities as abject. This is not simply about whether these subjects remain in a position of abjection but rather about sorting through the conditions that make that meaning shift. The political impetus is that one cannot have a different meaning unless the value ascribed changes. The lives of mad people matter. Black lives matter.

According to a linear progressive view of history, as the value of Blackness and madness increase, the abjection ascribed to them will dissipate or go away altogether. Indeed, the fiction of postracial discourse is that we are/were currently in this/that cultural moment. (The operative word here is fiction.) The conversations before this moment reveal that the artists-theorists discussed in this volume provide useful disruptions to linear time and progressive narratives. In drawing an intellectual cartography, this project lays bare how these artists-theorists trouble the stativity of those ideas and, in their dynamic theorizing, intervene in the commonly held discourses about Blackness and madness. As I warned, this map would uncover, recover, and discover, at times, contradictory relationships in the folds, lingering in the cut. A small bit of redistricting: Octavia E. Butler's work wonders whether mutual constitution functions as an adroit reading strategy. Nalo Hopkinson suggests the intraracial space may offer some disruptive aesthetic and narrative potential, which challenges Butler without dismissing the possibility for new interpretative strategy. Tananarive Due's heuristic queries how either of the worlds Butler and Hopkinson craft became possible given the ideological concept of the human. Each conversation intertwines with the other to examine the fissures in our analyses of Blackness and madness. As a result, they raise questions about the sought after goals of understanding these narratives. In what follows, I endeavor to do what is perhaps impolite at the end of a conversation: crawl under the discussion to retrace a thread that subtends but possibly upends the entire enterprise. I ask, if the value of Black madness and mad Blackness increases, do Black madness and/or mad Blackness retain the same meanings?

This discussion follows from two critical impulses. First, as Michelle Wright points out, it is possible that one portion of a person's identity takes precedent over another in any given situation. When Blackness is understood as a product of epiphenomenal time, rather than linear time, "the 'now' is *foregrounded* by agency because Blackness begins as its own interpellation in the moment."[1] In a room full of Black women, Blackness does not lose value—in point of fact, its heightened value may be the basis for the gathering—but it changes meaning. Other facets of identity spring to the fore: socioeconomic position, queer identity, gender identification, ability status, faith, educational background, geopolitical origin, size, occupation, political commitments, and the list continues. Thinking through fluctuating identities within Blackness or madness is not only an ordinary occurrence but, because of its commonplace nature, is vitally necessary to produce scholarship that includes the myriad groups that fall under the categories in question. As disability studies scholar Pauline Eyre echoes, "As I move about my daily life, my disability shifts in value according to the perceptions of me belonging to those to whom I relate. Not only does my impaired body affect my way of behaving *ab initio* but it also has differing effects on the relationships that make up my life."[2] In other words, the meanings of identities shift according to social and power dynamics, and exert differing pressures on any given interaction. The intersection is busy. Second, I grow concerned about what happens when we attend to changing values accrued to mad Black and Black mad subjects. To be fair, increased value and all that it entails—a radical shift in legal, political, social, technological, and cultural discursive and built spaces—still remains a long way off. That is, if value increases and meaning does not change, then we remain mired in a set of paradigms that view the mad Black or the Black mad only as abject. Even if one acknowledges this valuation system as bankrupt (which I certainly think it is), we must both theoretically and practically figure out how to make room for and sense meanings other than abjection. Say, joy and pleasure.

In this discussion, the novel emerges as one fecund space to explore the relationship between meaning and value, since it is a genre where the mad Black and the Black mad have traditionally occupied complicated positions. Since this conversation stops (Note: I do not think an ending is possible) a book on reconceptualizing Black madness and mad Blackness, it strikes me that a turn to the novel could be at the very least unexpected and, at worst, jejune. Elsewhere in this project, I have discussed novels, but I turn to the novel as a genre for how it as an ideological product participates in creating meaning and value.[3] I also turn to the novel because of how Mat Johnson's theorization of the Black novel form and tradition in his criticism and craft reconfigures the conversations elsewhere in this project. Further, the novel pushes this project beyond the tradition of Black speculative fiction to understand madness and Blackness in other contexts. As andré carrington reminds us, Black speculative fiction creates myriad refracted Blacknesses.

Any consideration of Black literature would be unwise to delimit the conversations about those refracted Blacknesses (of which madness is a part) to solely Black speculative fiction, since, as he notes, the genre is not alone in contemplating various forms of Blackness.[4] I concede the point that a discussion of the novel marks a turn toward an enterprise that often exercises its might against the mad Black or the Black mad subject. Yet, I want to reckon with the fact that all the artists-theorists discussed so far have chosen to work within this form. It offers narrative space, and typically for a mad Black subject, safer space for complexity often ignored or willfully dismissed.[5]

Pulling from my earlier ruminations on mutual constitution, it is here in the novel that these subjects are not merely crafted by the world around them. They cannot be wholly recuperative or radical. Rather, this is potentially (though not exclusively) the space where they constitute everything else, where they embrace "the indecorous paradox, to have a creative doctrine that insists upon sickness instead of curing it."[6] For all that the novel offers artistically, it also requires an engagement with the linear progressive narrative — via complicity or critique — and Western conceptions of rationality — again, via complicity or critique. Moreover, for disability studies scholars who shun examining disability solely with an eye toward metaphor, it offers the possibility of discomfort that accompanies absorption into another's interiority. In Michael Bérubé's article, "Disability and Narrative," a scholarly appetizer to his book *The Secret Life of Stories*, he implores literary scholars to think and analyze disability beyond the figurative. While he finds merit in the idea that disability can and should be representational, he understands it to act much in the way I have already described in this text — as a combination of metaphor, representation, critique, commentary, and aesthetic enterprise. Sami Schalk's work expands this idea by pinpointing that Black contexts often require viewing materiality and metaphor simultaneously, a point with which Dennis Tyler Jr. agrees when addressing the historical context of late nineteenth- and early twentieth-century Black engagements with Blackness and disability.[7] Linking these scholars in conversation, I find that an analysis of what the novel can do is not just merely apropos, but vitally necessary. Certainly, as the previous discussions have shown, a novel can be mad Black — can aesthetically and narratologically eschew linearity and ocularity — but the question remains as to what this form of looking, reading, and analyzing offers in terms of shifting the meanings of Blackness and madness.

I mine these tensions within the work of Mat Johnson: author of four novels, four graphic novels, one creative nonfiction historical account, and a particularly and delightfully active and sardonic Twitter feed. Johnson's work continues a Black novel tradition, often invoking his revered and earnest predecessors. Yet, Johnson's work carries with it the irreverence of some (satirical) predecessors such as George Schuyler and Fran Ross and contemporaries such as Percival Everett, Paul Beatty, Colson Whitehead, Alice Randall, and Danzy Senna. Across his oeuvre, Johnson has a penchant for depicting the mad Black character without resolving the issue their madness or Blackness precipitates. In other words, he foregoes the impulse to use madness as a "narrative prosthesis" in which disability prompts the action or problem of the novel but disappears as the action takes place.[8] His mad Black characters do not take a subordinate role to other more important characters, nor does he disappear their disability within supposedly more important story lines. Here, he crystallizes that "words on disability are themselves a doing."[9] Johnson has much in common with the other artists-theorists in this conversation, even though some of his work would not be considered speculative fiction. Nonetheless, Johnson's irreverence vis-à-vis time, space, and reason places him among his speculative fiction peers as one who theorizes about possibilities of a mad Blackness delinked from abjection. Though his literary corpus relies on some of the tools of traditional speculative fiction—Faustian bargains, time travel, alternative universes, monsters—Johnson's work permits my discussion to pan outward, bearing repercussions beyond those for whom speculative fiction is their primary medium.[10]

Two questions drive my curiosity here. First, how does a shift away from abjection as a primary meaning of Blackness and madness transform the value of each? (Implicit in this question are "Can it?" and "Will it?") Second, how does the Black novel form and tradition intervene in changing the meanings of mad Blackness and Black madness? I wheel through this inquiry by examining Johnson's meditation on the novel as incomplete but truthful. Then I turn to Johnson's second novel—*Hunting in Harlem* (2003)—because there he theorizes about readers' participation: Black madness and mad Blackness change meaning and/or value depending on who reads the text. Here, the mad Black and the Black mad disrupt the novel form, revealing its inherent incompleteness. This novel requires participation to determine what and where the stakes of the texts lie: as Shoshana Felman states, "The most scandalous thing about this scandalous story is that *we are forced to participate in the scandal,* that the reader's innocence cannot remain intact: there is no such thing as an innocent reader of this text."[11] In this way, Johnson lays bare that a mad Black/Black mad subject gets authored by an environment in which value and meaning both perform one of three functions: it can be ascribed to, possibly resisted by, or acquiesced to by a character.[12] In Johnson's novels, mad Black and Black mad subjects are not obstreperous issues or characters that need to be resolved. Instead, they point to the inability to resolve a novel when one is fixated on the wrong problem. That is, Johnson's narratives force readers to determine how they might author a character as mad or Black or both (ascribe meaning) and, therefore, decide whether they intend to reach for the pleasant but violent fictions of whiteness and ability as normal and desirable (ascribe value). The novel as an ideological and pedagogical project forces readers to participate through their interpretation. In so doing, they make decisions about meanings of madness and Blackness based on the value they ascribe to them. Like the critics discussed earlier (perhaps they are the same), the readers reveal themselves to themselves, exposing fissures in interpretation, gaps created by discrepancies between meaning and value.

Considering the Novel

Johnson's commentary on the novel veers slightly away from his usually sardonic writerly persona to offer a more sobering (and perhaps reverent) view of the form. Tasked with the foreword to a critical collection, *Contemporary African American Literature: The Living Canon* (2013) edited by the late Lovalerie King and Shirley Moody-Turner, Johnson laments the existence of a social media (Facebook) group called "I Hate Reading." Though he bemoans this as a writer, he states that he understands this personally, since novels are hard to read.[13] The reason for this difficulty is that "novels are incomplete in their process, forcing the reader to use her or his imagination to bring the text to life."[14] In the rest of the essay, Johnson plants his feet firmly in the ambivalent posture of continuing to advocate for the novel while understanding (though falling short of endorsing) the reason why readers veer away from it. Johnson offers up Nabokov's *Lolita* as his example of how the novel "offers truth the best chance."[15] For the opening of a critical volume dedicated to contemporary African American literature, Johnson's example appears strange and offensive, since it links Humbert Humbert's pedophilic truth with the experiences of Blackness as another truth. The offense relies on configuring pedophilia in common colloquial terms as unethical and immoral, and also mobilizing madness as both an explanation for pedophilia and as a rationale for dismissing pedophiles. The implicit link between madness in this form and Blackness as represented by its literary output gets too close to suggesting parity between the two, and suggesting sexual deviancy as constitutive of Blackness itself. The irreverent point of his link indexes the incompleteness of the novel as a way for readers to determine which truths (lowercase "t") they are willing to accept. Johnson does not necessarily trust readers to gravitate toward the uncomfortable truths of Black literature, but he does trust the novel to offer them. And, since both parties require accountability, he opens the floor to critics to participate in the conversation. (It need not be missed that, as an artist-theorist himself, he also offers accountability to the critics as well.)

Without carrying forth the association between Blackness and sexual deviance,[16] I read Johnson's link between *Lolita* and Black novels as an imperfect, fraught analogy designed to pinpoint how provocative the novel form can be, particularly in Black literature. Despite Johnson's general proclivity toward the flippant in his writing, I opt to take him somewhat seriously here, keeping in mind that his irreverence should shadow this discussion, a critical Cheshire cat grinning while disappearing, if you will. If Johnson is serious, the recourse to *Lolita* marshals the absurd critical and commercial success of a novel that sides with a man who by his own standards (and others') is an ethical and moral failure. Johnson suggests that, if Nabokov can succeed in this endeavor, Black literature—for all of the resistance it faces—should not be so summarily dismissed. If one reads Johnson's foreword as tongue-in-cheek, his comparison foregrounds the fact that a large portion of the reading public for Black literature has been exposed to (or may even believe in) the racist supposition that Blacks are inherently sexually deviant (another way to believe in the conflation of certain kinds of madnesses and Blacknesses). Note that the option to read Johnson as earnest or not opens up the same space of interpretive possibility as his novels. In the spirit of interpretive oscillation that this discussion courts, one must decide one's own stakes and interpretive strategies as a way to settle (albeit uncomfortably) on the significance and implications of his critical ideas. Devouring the truths within Black novels may be—regardless of the opinions of authors, advocates, or critics—a similar experience to reading Humbert Humbert. Invoking Nabokov as part of a loose analogy continues to venerate the Black novel tradition (Nabokov was short-listed for the National Book Award in fiction, after all) even as it requires a shift in perspective about how the tradition of Black letters functions. The novel form's offer of truth, then, is a vexed one—it allows only for the truth readers are ready to accept, the meanings they already acknowledge, the values they already hold.

The Black novel tradition has the capacity to shift the meaning of various kinds of Blacknesses, including those that intersect with madness. Yet, this tradition must account for the way Blackness intertwines with histories of colonialism, imperialism, and slavery. How is it that one can acknowledge that Blackness is not "produced *only* as a result of traumatizing violent domination and historical defeats [and] grapple further with that apparently inescapable *aspect* of Blackness . . . described by terms such as defeat, violation, and humiliation?"[17] To do so requires an assiduous retooling of the terms of Blackness itself without eliding history. The Black novel tradition has sought to problematize, explain, revise, and upend the ideology that gives Black abjection the heft of its meaning.[18] In the words of Christina Sharpe, the Black novel lives "in the wake" similar to Black subjects: "even as we experienced, recognized, and lived subjection, we did not *simply* or *only* live *in* subjection and *as* the subjected."[19] Much like the critical theorists in a previous discussion (see the third conversation), Black novelists (dealing with the constraints of genre and historical moment) critique how Blackness comes to equal abjection and under what conditions this might change. Some reach the nihilistic conclusion that it won't, and others provide scenarios wherein Blackness becomes more than the sum total of history accrued to it. On either side of the ideological spectrum, novels contend with the constraint of how history makes meaning. They must either change history or reimagine it.

In Johnson's novels, he asserts his challenge to wholesale Black abjection with the figure of the mad Black, with all that entails in terms of disrupting Western lineages of linearity and ocularity. As I mentioned, Johnson deploys the mad Black without resorting to the oft-used technique of thinking through this character as a problem in need of resolution. Though I will not discuss all of his novels, these figures surface in each of his putatively traditional novels: *Drop* (2001), *Hunting in Harlem* (2003), *Pym* (2012), and *Loving Day* (2015). At times, they are secondary (or ghostly) characters, as is the case with *Drop* and *Loving Day*. In *Hunting in Harlem* and *Pym*, the main characters shoulder the histories of mad Blackness in their quests for pleasure or peace. Johnson's graphic novels tend toward exploiting others' perceptions of an idea as irrational as they undermine the foundations for those perceptions. *Papa Midnite* (2006) disrupts the idea that to strive for Black freedom automatically indicates madness. *Incognegro* (2008) and *Right State* (2012) refashion the relationships between state power, violence, and Blackness, mobilizing the absurdity of race as recognizable by the unimpeachability of sight.[20] *Dark Rain* (2010) is one of Johnson's more traditional graphic novels—including a jewel heist and a redemptive figure—but it examines how grief, state violence, incarceration, and poverty create the racialized and sanist realities that some might consider irrational or crazy. Johnson's creative historical nonfiction, *The Great Negro Plot* (2007), mines the history of New York City's enslaved populations to pinpoint how white fear and racism create the contemporary (ir)rational world. In all of his work, Johnson privileges the supposedly irrational while reckoning with the history that has wrought it. Loath to broach conclusions, Johnson proffers a way of rethinking how, why, where, and when Blackness and madness make meanings other than abjection.

Piques of Absurdity

Mat Johnson's critical work opens up the possibility for viewing the fluctuating relationship between value and meaning. His foreword suggests that increased valuation of Blackness must reckon with the influence of history and abjection within the Black novel tradition if it is to offer some kind of truth (however incomplete). Given his use of mad Black characters, Johnson's work implies that madness and Blackness work in tandem to alter meaning. His second novel, *Hunting in Harlem*, features a character whose mad Blackness determines how we read Johnson's text and the entire tradition (by Johnson's implication). *Hunting in Harlem* follows the lives of three ex-offenders as they attempt reentry through the Horizon Realty's Second Chance Program. Ostensibly, the program's founder, Cyrus Marks, aims to provide them with on-the-job training so that they can "become something more."[21] However, the protagonist, Cedric Snowden, learns that Horizon Realty actually implicates the three men in a nefarious gentrification plot, realized by killing so-called undesirable residents (pickpockets, drug lords, and pedophiles) to create vacancies for upwardly mobile Black people. Since the third-person omniscient narrator principally focuses on Snowden, the text delays revealing Horizon's murderous plan until Snowden learns of it. One of the other ex-offenders, Bobby Finley (the character who is my focus here), appears to understand before Snowden does. Despite Bobby's acquiescence, he continues to voice moral objections to the plan. The novel ends with Bobby's suicide by self-immolation on a rooftop, which ironically ensures the success and proliferation of Horizon's gentrification scheme.

Bobby Finley's character permits multiple interpretations of the novel. What determines whether those analyses work is a reader's relationship to the meanings of mad Blackness Bobby represents. The narrator, in maintaining a vexed position vis-à-vis Bobby, allows one to oscillate regarding how Bobby makes meaning. For instance, the narrator keeps a fair distance by describing him mostly as awkward or remarking on his ideas (through other characters or through narration) as ridiculous. Snowden keeps him at a distance. Yet, the narration also confirms Bobby's observations such that he, at times, appears prescient. For instance, he is the first to voice objection to Horizon Realty's plans. He becomes a laughable and somewhat pathetic character whose ambitions, including his romantic ones, remain feeble and awkward in comparison to the more sure-footed Snowden or the more aggressive Horus (the third ex-offender). Until Bobby decides to light himself on fire, he evinces a fair amount of fragility in the face of his employer's plot to revitalize Harlem. In the descriptions of his interiority, Bobby appears to oscillate between fear, pyromania, and skepticism. The narration regularly keeps his fears (often legitimate) at the periphery unless Snowden expresses them. Further, the descriptions of Bobby's future plans to become a successful writer affirm him, since those plans position him as the only one of the three interns who seeks a viable alternative to recidivism or forced abjection.[22] Snowden wants to disappear himself into his previous environs to live out his days as a landlord in Philadelphia. He has no start-up capital, no plan. This isn't limned as a bad idea, just not a feasible one. Horus embraces the realtor's plan with alacrity, seeming to enjoy the violence he metes out on behalf of the real estate agency. Whereas Snowden and Horus lean toward scenarios that court or create Black abjection, Bobby harnesses his interest in pyromania to foment an identity out of his artistic production.[23] To be clear, this is no less an engagement with Black abjection, but of a different sort than Horus or Snowden.

In tergiversating about Bobby's interiority, the narration poses an interpretive problem. Specifically, does one understand Bobby's mad Blackness as abject? Astute? His madness becomes the lens through which the reader could suspend disbelief and yet still be engaged with the action of the novel. If one ignores the narration's implication that Bobby's ideas are the slow creep of neurosis, then his fragility becomes a critique of the novel's irreverent premise of gentrification. Even in choosing one's interpretation of his madness, Bobby cannot be so easily discarded as either neurotic or fragile. Not only does he adroitly read the immorality of Horizon Realty's plans for Harlem, but he also points out the fungibility of the ex-convicts with regard to its plans. He gives voice to the possible objections to Horizon Realty since it jeopardizes his reach toward freedom. As a result, the novel does not disappear Bobby's awkwardness, nor does it mute his ambitions (romantic or writing). Instead, the scandal—to use Shoshana Felman's term—is that Bobby is the moral fulcrum point on which the novel leverages its critique of the gentrification process and the ideology that would excise certain inhabitants. Using Shoshana Felman's words and signifying on Ralph Ellison, "The joke is indeed on us; the worry, ours."[24]

Bobby operates as a fold for *Hunting in Harlem*: his mad Blackness becomes an oppositional, mercurial space from which to interpret the critique of the text vis-à-vis gentrification. Since the narration destabilizes the text through him, Bobby can intussuscept the novel such that multiple interpretations present themselves—even if their validity rests on the politics of the interpreter. Reading Bobby's writerly ambitions reveals a cut in the text. Specifically, his own relationship to other Black authors and his knowledge of history queries the relationship of the Blackness of his contemporary moment to the Blackness of Harlem past (circa 1900 to 1930). Bobby writes a tome humbly titled *The Great Work*, which as Snowden describes, numbs the mind because most of the 374 pages take place within a closet, and "much of the novel is description."[25] Bobby purposes "perhaps to underscore the uselessness of the English language to capture this environment" so "going neither up nor down, unassisted by plot or question, the prose is forced to crawl forward word by word, digging deliberately for purchase. No matter how quickly one reads *The Great Work*, the process never feels a moment less than seven months."[26] *The Great Work*'s scandal is its insistent use of the word snow, "so many times that the reader becomes so numb from it."[27] The novel also emphasizes description rather than plot such that these two elements have the effect of prolonging time itself. Of course, the narrator's description here, ventriloquized through Snowden's interiority, ridicules Bobby's novel and Bobby himself. His failure insinuates that the novel form in Black letters serves a particular purpose. Its so-called truth cannot be about craft or the natural world. Instead, the meanings of Blackness are delimited such that one cannot value Bobby's book. Or, given the satirical thrust of Johnson's novel, Bobby's failure could imply the opposite.

Here, Bobby's relationship with writing invaginates Johnson's novel, since it points to the desire for Black abjection within a Black novel tradition. The presence of Bobby's novel questions the expectations of a (Black) public that reads (Black) books. What kinds of experiences do they desire to read, and what is their tolerance of works that do not meet these expectations? Bobby's novel not only "refuses summarization, defiantly,"[28] but it also denies the reader the oft-written styles of Black novels: social realism, protest, memoir, bildungsroman, or even speculative fiction. Instead, Bobby's *The Great Work* takes the form of a man-versus-nature tale where the protagonist is alone and must carry the narrative by himself.[29] Bobby's fictional novel asks all who read it to make a decision about whether they will become part of the snowy cold it describes and the character who has to bear it. Given Bobby's abysmal sales (he decides to purchase all copies of his book because he believes no one appreciates it), it would appear that out of boredom or disinterest, readers have chosen not to engage because the novel does not describe a world they inhabit. Various characters' engagement with it suggests that Black readers define good literature based on abject Black experience and a desire that those narratives affirm Black abjection. Bobby's relationship to the publication process foregrounds how engagement with his novel (and by extension Johnson's novel and the tradition they represent) seems to require an orientation toward seeing oneself in the text. For Bobby, the inability to see oneself in his text indicates stupidity: he calls readers who do not appreciate his work dung beetles (mostly Black women) and names his toilet Irving Howe so that he can happily defecate in it daily. The natural corollary of Bobby's opinion is that (Black) readers of (Black) novels lack the imaginative capacity to think of Blackness in terms other than abjection.

Again, Bobby's character forces one to decide—based on the narrative one wishes to believe about his mad Blackness—whether he should be dismissed because his mad Blackness constitutes abjection. Or does Bobby's mad Blackness, in its increase in value vis-à-vis the text (that is, you need it for interpretation), move away from abjection? If Bobby is right and a Black reading public does not wish to be or to read anything other than Black degradation, then the central question of Johnson's novel becomes less urgent: can one vivify Harlem in any way without doing violence to its citizenry? To be clear, Johnson's double entendre within the title—where "hunting" points not only to the colloquial phrase related to an apartment search but also to the stalking required in the relationship between predator and prey—implies that Johnson's novel has already decided that gentrification is undoubtedly a violent process. Here, the revivification process assumes a death of the citizenry that is not corroborated by reality (until one of the ex-offenders kills someone). Abjection and the desire for it, then, justifies gentrification within the world of the novel. Yet, Bobby's experience with the novel, since the narration vacillates about endorsing him, suggests that Johnson's irreverent premise forms a valid critique: the idea that gentrification-as-improvement requires ex-convicts to murder putative undesirables provides and preempts the rationale usually given for neighborhood improvement endeavors. Bobby's metatextuality brings into sharp relief the urgency of Johnson's work not only because it problematizes the desire for Black abjection but also because it relies on the catastrophe of Black abjection to make its critique. Johnson's novel does not have the frozen tundra as a setting. It does not take place in solitude. It bears real-life implications for people currently living in Harlem (and other similarly situated geopolitical spaces). Yet, Johnson's work (generally) "disowns and savages . . . ideology itself as a means toward desirable ends" as a way to satirize "Black people in their own environs."[30] Not only is the ideology behind gentrification unsafe from critique, but so is the purported desire behind reading Black novels that explicitly deal with systemic oppression. Here is the invagination of the text, the space where the world of the novel, the world outside, and the idea of the text collide and implode: despite the urgency of *Hunting in Harlem*'s critique, the novel—through Bobby—suggests that readers' pleasure lies in reading about, assuaging themselves with, and thereby continuing stories of Black degradation.[31]

So what lies within this fold?

As with most of his satirical work, Johnson performs the role of diagnostician without offering a viable solution. He equivocates about the capacity of the novel form to offer truth in this context given the meanings ascribed to Bobby's mad Blackness. Within the text, Bobby's suicide leaves the novel elliptically open, since his new self-published book (about his fictional relationship with love interest, Piper Goines) sells remarkably well and the Horizon Realty project expands. Rather than receive the neat ending in which good triumphs over evil, Johnson provides an open ending, one that queries how gentrification happens now. The novel concludes with Bobby's suicide, a mass impetus to purchase his second book, and Snowden as the new face of Horizon Realty's ever-expanding violent gentrification scheme. Enfolded in this is the question of what *Hunting in Harlem* invites one to believe about the possibilities of mad Black narratives more broadly. The reader has to make a set of analytical decisions about their interpretative strategies, all of which bear implications for the meanings of Blackness and madness. One has to make a choice: Bobby's uneasiness about arson, his awkward behavior, and his eventual suicide foreclose the possibility that one can remain innocently detached from the world Johnson's narrator describes. To believe Bobby, or at least to give room for his opinion and existence, questions the possibility of gentrification and revitalization. To disbelieve him is to disavow knowledge of the connections and objections he raises about the carceral system, revitalization, and citizenship. Either choice reveals a set of political opinions and stakes.

Here, *Hunting in Harlem* inquires about the neatness of the narratives one tells oneself (or one is willing to be told) about Blackness and madness. Allowing that Bobby Finley's writing exceeds the boundaries of the text and refuses easy reconciliation, his madness about Blackness exploits the neatness expected of a Black novel by revealing that the abjection on which it relies requires participation from a reading public. Bobby Finley–as-intussusception spotlights that Black abjection has some basis in historical fact. In this way, Bobby facilitates the iconoclasm within *Hunting in Harlem*: the venerability of a Black novel tradition based on Black abjection and consumed by a (mostly) white readership.[32] Bobby's failure to launch his first novel (and the expected success of his second posthumous novel) suggests that the Black novel tradition occupies a vexed space that must include abjection even if it attempts to trouble its influence. Further, Johnson's novel clarifies that the neat narrative is an assumption at the crux of understanding the novel as a bound, enclosed, material object and an ideological construct. In order for the novel to function as a product of Enlightenment thought, a manifestation of and catering to the sanist, white, masculine ideal of the human, it must tell neat (in all its valences as orderly, pleasing, and practiced) stories. Yet, Johnson's novel acts as its own Cheshire cat, grinning while disappearing. Through Bobby's mad Blackness and Johnson's own mad Black aesthetic, *Hunting in Harlem* toys with what it means to interpret and analyze in the fold of mad Black abjection. Recall that madness and Blackness both get authored by a public that takes for granted their synonymous relationship with excess and abjection. *Hunting in Harlem* opens up the space for Bobby and the novel to be multivalenced based on a reader's relationship to madness and Blackness. In so doing, Johnson intimates that the incomplete truth of the novel, what his mad Black novel offers, reflects the valuation given by a reading public and that public's understanding of what and how mad Blackness and Black madness come to mean.

Like the other artists-theorists discussed here, Johnson only allows me to crawl crab-wise toward answering my initial inquiries. As I mentioned, I deliberately explore a shift away from abjection as a primary meaning for Blackness and madness: whether it can happen and whether the valuation of each changes. I am also interested in how the Black novel form intervenes in this endeavor. Regarding the latter, Johnson hints that the answer is "It depends on the reader." If, as he suggests, the novel is fundamentally incomplete and the Black novel's incompleteness relies on the world it inhabits, then readers may interpret the novels however they see fit, based on how they value madness and Blackness. Regarding the former question, Johnson offers a more nuanced response. To be fair, this is no less a Cheshire cat grinning and disappearing than either his criticism or his fiction. Johnson mobilizes Bobby's knowledge of history and the layered referential nature of satire to exploit the complicated nexus of history, literature, and abjection. In one scene, Bobby begrudgingly goes to a Horizon Realty evening event during which he and Piper Goines spend time discussing his work and her life. While on Mount Morris with the other guests, Bobby chooses to impress Piper with his knowledge of Harlem's literary landscape. He asks, "Do you remember that Mount Morris Park was where the main character did the eulogy in *Invisible Man*?"[33] He proceeds to tell her the history of the hill—formerly called Slang Berg (Snake Hill) in Dutch and renamed by the brownstone's original realtors—and points out the places where the Dutch used to look out for fires. He points to an iron crow's nest above them, citing, "That was built to look for fires, since this is one of the highest vantage points in Manhattan."[34] He then goes on to point out other landmarks significant to Black cultural history in Harlem: a building in Sugar Hill where Langston Hughes lived, and the residences of W. E. B. Du Bois, Alain Locke, and Zora Neale Hurston, among others.[35]

Bobby's spatial positioning suggests a particularly vexed relationship to New York's (and other geopolitical spaces') layered histories of enslavement, surveillance, literary triumph, and celebration. Drawing on the figurative meaning embedded in the "stories of the buildings," Bobby's brief history links the surveillance of the Dutch fires to Black cultural history to his contemporary moment. His own position of surveillance troubles the idea that he can look backward at history and see it clearly. In a literal sense, he is above the residences but below the crow's nest. In a figurative sense, he is beholden to both. This challenges a historical narrative of progression by signaling his possible relationship to each moment in history: still under surveillance that began in the eighteenth century and building on the lives of New Negro Movement figures. Bobby's knowledge troubles the idea that history is truly in the past and that building on top of it (literally or figuratively) will result in erasing it. More important to this discussion, this scene in *Hunting in Harlem* signals the extent to which Black novels struggle with and revise narratives about the past. In that moment, *Hunting in Harlem* links Dutch surveillance of the city, Bobby's surveillance of Horizon Realty's murderous plans for gentrification, and Harlem's cultural history. At its most sardonic, the text suggests that the violence of gentrification and maintenance of the city is not altogether new but rather a logical pattern in New York. By spatially positioning the contemporary moment (Bobby) between the eighteenth century (crow's nest) and the early twentieth century (famous Harlem residences), the text also troubles the pattern. The twenty-first century stands in the gap created by the stories built upon and the stories to which one is still subordinate. Despite Bobby's clear spatial positioning above one and below the other, it is not necessarily true that he is solely beholden to a history of Dutch enslavement and surveillance or building on Harlem literary giants. The histories are also reversible. He has built on Dutch histories of enslavement and surveillance (especially given his participation in Horizon Realty's program), and he remains subordinate to Harlem's literary giants (given his desired literary relationship to them).

As if to punctuate this idea, Piper Goines's name invokes another author whose legacy intertwines abjection, triumph, celebration, and tragedy: Donald Goines. Donald Goines (published under Al C. Clark) wrote popular fiction books, particularly the Kenyatta series, which participates in the same irreverence about Black radical ideology, criminalization, and revivification as Johnson. In *Crime Partners* (1978), *Death List* (1974), *Kenyatta's Escape* (1974), and *Kenyatta's Last Hit* (1975), Goines writes about a Black radical organization (loosely based on the Black Panthers) that seeks to change the urban community by getting rid of crime. Though Piper does not advocate violence and, in fact, becomes a victim of it herself (meted out by Horus), her connection to Goines signals another kind of relationship to Black (literary) histories. Namely, Donald Goines's novels speak to a desire to reimagine Blackness and Black spaces, giving value to oft denigrated components of Black life while also complicating the meanings accrued to them. Yet, if Piper invokes not only Goines's work but also Goines's life, then his violent (and unsolved) death may also imply the impossibility of that task.

Johnson's novel mobilizes the heavily referential nature of satire and Bobby's mad Blackness to mark the novel's incompleteness, that which is offered "within the darkened space of your imagination, [where] anything can be said, any truth can be uttered, with intimacy."[36] Bobby's vexed position vis-à-vis history suggests that valuing Blackness and madness differently does not automatically shift the meanings thereof away from abjection. He has to reckon with history first, and, in that moment, he finds himself—as do others, by implication—awkwardly positioned between the past and the present, living in the gap. Since it is through Bobby Finley that one determines how to read the text, it is his conception of history that authors meaning and ascribes value. In true pyromaniacal fashion, he consumes history and seeks to purify it. The embers, if you will, evidence that one cannot proceed without an attention to history. It lingers, smolders. The oblique reference to Donald Goines suggests the possibility of reading history and literature countermnemonically with an eye toward the mercurial and radical even if the result is not revolution. Given that Goines was based in Detroit, invoking him also signals a broader geopolitical reach. Johnson's meditations in *Hunting in Harlem* ruminate on the same ideas as within Butler's *Fledgling*: namely, how do we read recuperation or resistance in a space mired in histories of abjection? Due's heuristic interjects here as well to theorize about the critical possibilities available when the concept of the human loses its luster. If *Hunting in Harlem* proposes remaining in the gap as an avenue toward interpretation, then the human cannot retain the same critical purchase. Circling back to Hopkinson, this conversation also warns that we not elide the places where mad Blackness can be destructive or create abjection as well. Certainly, this critiques the notion that Black fiction functions as merely sociological treatise, an issue that other scholars have already taken up with aplomb.[37] Abjection, then, is not the incomplete truth the Black novel tradition needs to or seeks to avoid. Instead, it becomes part of—not primarily or exclusively—the creating and the theorizing.

Value's Meaning and Meaning's Value:
Ending without Concluding

This book is uncorrected proof. You read it
on your eyelids. You sleep under it.
You give it away. You tear out whole chapters.
You say you read it but you didn't.

— Morgan Parker, "The Book of Negroes,"
There Are More Beautiful Things Than Beyoncé

What of the linear progressive narrative that attempts to discipline Black madness and mad Blackness into being valuable but meaningless? At first blush, it appears to propose a more just world. It suggests that we are moving toward a historical moment that recognizes difference but does not attach abrogated meaning to it: at the end of time, we will shed the meanings of our bodies. Yet, the repercussions for such a world, even the desires for that world, require willful incursions into an ideological territory that demands anti-Blackness and ableism as its governing principles. Making meaning is not merely an intellectual exercise. It rightfully establishes Blackness and madness as integral parts of history, clarifying that their existence as abject has been crucial to creating and sustaining the violent fictions of whiteness and ability as normal. And that their objection to abjection has been and remains disruptive.

It is in the nature of a conclusion to wrap up or sum up a story already told, but in the story of madness and Blackness, we've already seen that Black madness :: mad Blackness exceeds the boundaries of a text. It then becomes impossible to create an apt conclusion for this kind of work. Consider this veritable lack of conclusion a mark of this project's own mad Blackness. Each conversation in this volume unpacks the various meanings and critical interpretive strategies available when madness and Blackness intersect. As I mentioned before, the conversations here take for granted that critics and creatives speak to each other, complicate one another's ideas. For that reason, I read the gaps each leaves open in their conversations with one another. I mine the tensions and deferrals, the mercurial and the transformative possibilities of the fold and the flesh. What appears in this volume attends to how Black madness :: mad Blackness upends, destabilizes. My wayward project demonstrates that an exploration of this sort often raises more questions than it answers, or, as was often the case in the previous discussions, does not allow a direct answer at all. How do we push the two fields together if mutual constitution is not altogether useful? What occurs when madness is a Black thang but eschews culturally nationalist leanings? Why might it be impossible to get outside the confines of the human? How does the venerable Black novel tradition offer a challenge to linear progressive temporal understanding? What becomes clear is that one cannot get beyond either madness or Blackness but rather must find the spaces where excess, unknowability, and insanity do not account for them in all their complexity.

The only way out is through.

FIGURE 4.1 This image is intended as a provocation, another cover to an as yet unwritten work. *Black Madness :: Mad Blackness* chooses not to conclude, suggesting that these conversations are necessarily ongoing. Wangechi Mutu; *Riding Death in My Sleep*, 2002. Ink and collage on paper; 60 × 44 in. Courtesy of the Artist and Peter Norton.

PREFACE

1 Several book reviews have pointed out the utility of the work within the fields with which it is engaged and places where the project could have gone further. See Fadda, "Review of *New Body Politics: Narrating Arab and Black Identity in the Contemporary United States*," Harb, "Review of *New Body Politics: Narrating Arab and Black Identity in the Contemporary United States*," Kafer, "Review of *New Body Politics: Narrating Arab and Black Identity in the Contemporary United States*," Khrebtan-Hörhager, "Review of *New Body Politics: Narrating Arab and Black Identity in the Contemporary United States*," and Vedere, "Review of *New Body Politics: Narrating Arab and Black Identity in the Contemporary United States*."

2 This insight became more apparent after I read Brittney Cooper's *Beyond Respectability*. I thank her profoundly for her labor in laying that bare. See Cooper, *Beyond Respectability: The Intellectual Thought of Race Women*, 11–32.

3 For other works where I have used this strategy, see Pickens, "The Verb Is No"; "What Drives Work"; and "Blue Blackness, Black Blueness."

4 Christian, "Race for Theory," 288.

5 Trethewey, "Thrall," 59.

INTRODUCTION

1 Kriegel, "Uncle Tom and Tiny Tim."

2 Kriegel, "Uncle Tom and Tiny Tim."

3 Kriegel, "Uncle Tom and Tiny Tim."

4 This occurs in scholarship that is primarily about race but includes a discussion of dismemberment, embodiment, or mental illness without exploring

disability studies angles. This occurs in scholarship that is primarily about disability, but only includes a discussion of race as tangential or in reference to something else wherein the scholarship about race has only a footnote or a brief citation.

5   Bradley Lewis's project generally asks the two fields of literature and medicine to speak to each other. He uses Chekov as a case study to think through the way we tell stories about depression. Though Lewis's work is useful for examining the way we narrativize medicine in fiction, I find it unhelpful for my purpose here: to expose how the discourses of race and disability broadly and madness and Blackness specifically transform one other. In *Depression*, he traces the etymology of melancholia and depression through Aristotle and Plato, finding that neither the humoral (Aristotle) nor the divinity (Plato) shy away from implicating Blackness as abject. As he describes the intellectual genealogy, Foucault takes up the Aristotelian understanding, thinking of humoral theory as the way depression is discursively constituted. As I explain in the methodological section of this introduction, melancholia and attendant humoral theories tend to cannibalize discussions about race since they allow little room for other ways of understanding the affect of depression (its causes, repercussions, etc.). This project is markedly different from that of Ann Cvetkovich, who ties depression to a set of cultural locations through affect theory. See Lewis, *Depression*; and Cvetkovich, *Depression*.

6   I choose to signify on Stevie Wonder's work for two reasons: first, as a Black blind musician, he often foregrounds the historical freight and psychoaffective weight of Blackness and disability in the public sphere. Second, even though I do not focus on Blackness and physical disability, I do not want to miss how those discussions have paved the way for my own work. One such discussion would be Terry Rowden's book on Blackness and blindness, *Songs of Blind Folk*.

7   Jarman, "Dismembering the Lynch Mob," 91.

8   In making this intellectual move to consider madness as socially constructed as well as materially bound, I lean on the legacy of Michel Foucault. Rather than rehearse Foucauldian arguments about the discourse of madness, I find it useful to point out that the scholarship upon which I more directly rely has Foucault's work on madness as a discursive construct as its foundation rendering such rehearsals and repetition unnecessary.

9   Most disability studies scholars who discuss mental or cognitive disability have some notations on language. I echo the sentiments of Margaret Price, who reminds us that no term is neutral in our discussions of psychiatric disability, mental illness, cognitive disability, intellectual disability, neurodiversity, neuroatypicality, psychiatric system survivors, mental health service users, craziness, and, of course, madness. Even though language acquires a particular urgency when discussing the mind, my aim to use mad recognizes the complex history the term carries as well as the full expansiveness of its lexical range. See Price, *Mad at School*.

10 Menzies, LeFrançois, and Reaume, *Mad Matters*, 10.

11 Sass, *Madness and Modernism*, 1.

12 Aho, Ben-Moshe, and Hilton, "Mad Futures," 294.

13 Aho, Ben-Moshe, and Hilton, "Mad Futures," 294.

14 It is also true that discussions of Blackness cannot and should not slide easily across cultural borders. For this reason, I choose not to engage Sander Gilman's work. In the chapter that appears in *On Blackness without Blacks* (1982) and, largely unchanged, in *Difference and Pathology* (1985), when he connects the degeneracy associated with Black sexuality to a discussion of Freud and race, it is in service of a discussion of Jewishness. It collapses the significant differences between the way race functions for Jewishness and Blackness. Though he understands that a common feature of Blackness and madness combined is a fear of the other's potential destruction and wildness, he neglects to think through how Blackness has more than just phobogenic potential. Useful for my purposes in this argument is his historical discussion of how Black Americans were implicated in the US census of 1840 as more insane than their (free) white counterparts. Gilman's explanations of madness also do not complicate the work of mad studies scholars who are, useful for my purposes, interested in defanging biopsychiatric definitions of madness and institutional instantiations thereof of their significant narrative and political power. Gilman's historical exploration of madness in art as a repressed secret in *Picturing Health and Illness* (1995) and madness as a cultural fantasy of ugliness in *Disease and Representation* (1988) are each incorporated in my understanding of madness as a slippery discourse that finds its way into multiple cultural locations. Such an understanding of madness as unruly undergirds my desire to mobilize artists-theorists to dialogue with and challenge critics.

15 Pickens, "Modern Family," 131.

16 Erevelles, "Crippin' Jim Crow," 87.

17 Gorman, "Quagmires of Affect," 312.

18 Schalk, "Interpreting Disability Metaphor and Race," 141.

19 Dennis Tyler Jr.'s article "Jim Crow's Disabilities: Racial Injury, Immobility, and the 'Terrible Handicap' in the Literature of James Weldon Johnson" also identifies how this slippage functions in the early twentieth century. According to Tyler, Johnson mobilizes disability as metaphor and materiality to underscore how it functions in determining who is legible as Black and white.

20 Barr, "All at One Point," xi.

21 During the review process, one reader pointed out that the double colon is also commonly used to introduce emotion or affect into a written conversation (i.e., :: blinks innocently ::) either to add genuine emotion or snark. Though that usage is less evocative for me here since it requires book-ending phrases with the double colon, it does bear mentioning as a way that the double colon refuses to provide easy clarity.

22 Black Dance Studies scholar Takiyah Amin discussed the problems with a "contribution model" of engaging Blackness. Her point was that thinking of Blackness as a contribution erases the role it plays in creating through either Black

bodies or methodologies/praxis of Black creative/critical thinking. See Amin, "Beyond Hierarchy."

23 Siebers, *Disability Theory*, 26.

24 Davis, *End of Normal*, 1–15.

25 Kafer, *Feminist. Queer. Crip.*, 149.

26 Donaldson and Prendergast, "No Crying," 130.

27 Bérubé, *Secret Life of Stories*, 27. Margaret Price also makes this point when she notes that the terms used to describe madness writ large have embedded within them dehumanizing logics. See Price, *Mad at School*, 1–24.

28 These include but are not limited to Jay Dolmage, Stephanie Kerschbaum, Margaret Price, and Melanie Yergeau.

29 See Cartwright, "Diseases and Peculiarities" and Samuels, *Fantasies of Identification*. Michael Bérubé's *Secret Life of Stories* explores the idea that a character need not have an intellectual disability for intellectual disability to affect the action of the text. Given the history of Blackness in the United States, I wager that this idea has been consistently at work in Black literature since its inception. This is one of the points hinted at in Christopher M. Bell's "Introducing White Disability Studies" as well.

30 Titchkosky, *Reading and Writing Disability Differently*, 40.

31 Bell, *Blackness and Disability*, 3.

32 T. Carey, *Rhetorical Healing*, 20.

33 V. Smith, "Loopholes of Retreat."

34 I would be remiss if I did not note the fact that there has been a recent explosion of scholarship on disability and race more broadly. Julie Avril Minich brings together the fields of Latinx studies and disability studies in her work *Accessible Citizenships: Disability, Nation, and the Cultural Politics of Greater Mexico* (2013), examining how Chicano/a communities mobilized disability as a way to expand the understanding of political community. Recent work in Indigenous studies and disability studies pinpoints that "disability was not always seen as such," but that some Indigenous cultures—I reference Siobhan Senier's work on Mohegan people in particular—understood disability as part of varied human experience (Senier, "Traditionally," 213–29). Eunjung Kim also explores disability in a Korean context in *Curative Violence: Rehabilitating Disability, Gender, and Sexuality in Modern Korea* (2017).

35 Morrison, *Playing in the Dark*, 3.

36 Suvin, "SF Novel in 1969," 158.

37 Darko Suvin develops a theory of science fiction in *Metamorphoses of Science Fiction*, clarifying that science fiction is not as far removed from realist fiction as one might desire to think. See Suvin, *Metamorphoses of Science Fiction*.

38 Lavender, *Race in Science Fiction*, 7; carrington, *Speculative Blackness*.

39 Butler, "Positive Obsession," 135.

40 Butler, "Positive Obsession," 134, 135.

41 My thinking in this regard comes from several locations, including Barbara Christian's "Race for Theory"; Ann Cvetkovich's *Depression*; and the late José

Esteban Muñoz memorial at the American Studies Association Minority Scholars breakfast. Rather than impose on scholars in their grief (though the Muñoz memorial speeches eloquently honored his work and were endlessly quotable), I choose to cite the work from which this idea came. See Christian, "Race for Theory"; Cvetkovich, *Depression*; and Muñoz, *Disidentifications*.

42 I borrow this term from Christina Sharpe's book of the same name in which she interprets the conditions that make violence fundamental to the New World Black subject. In her words, monstrous intimacies are "a set of known and unknown performances and inhabited horrors, desires and positions produced, reproduced, circulated, and transmitted that are breathed in like air and often acknowledged to be monstrous" (*Monstrous Intimacies*, 3). The novel, as I argue, is a monstrous, intimate space where disciplining violence gets enacted on bodies and subjects deemed nonnormative.

43 See Boster, *African American Slavery*; Cartwright, "Diseases and Peculiarities"; and Baynton, "Disability."

44 All of these could refer to multiple instances within the public sphere. However, one particular instance comes to mind. When officer Darren Wilson described his fatal encounter with Michael Brown, he described Brown as a demon, an unstoppable force that needed to be shot to be subdued. Officer Wilson shot and killed the eighteen-year-old Brown in Ferguson, Missouri, on August 9, 2014. Wilson was not indicted of killing Brown and was cleared of violating Brown's civil rights. In addition, the protesters who identified with the activist group Black Lives Matter were described as unreasonably angry and singularly discontent as opposed to understanding themselves as part of the long view of history. The reaction to non-Black allies was hostile and tended to question their sanity and intelligence. This is but one instance and is part of a larger pattern of using the associations with Blackness and madness to defang social and political critique. For Wilson's description, see Calamur, "Ferguson Documents."

45 Felman points out that madness is participatory in a few publications, notably *Writing and Madness: Literature/Philosophy/Psychoanalysis*, and in a section composed of three essays in *The Claims of Literature: A Shoshana Felman Reader*. Toni Morrison makes this point on multiple occasions, most notably in her critical text *Playing in the Dark* and with her short fiction "Recitatif."

46 Price, *Mad at School*, 141–75.

47 I discuss how this works in Mat Johnson's *Pym*. I point out how this discourse functions both in the fiction and in the academy. See Pickens, "Satire, Scholarship and Sanity."

48 Davis, *End of Normal*, 130.

49 See Nyong'o, *Amalgamation Waltz*.

50 Cheng, *Melancholy of Race*; Gilroy, *Postcolonial Melancholia*.

51 Edwards, *Charisma*, xvii; Kafer, *Feminist. Queer. Crip.*, 19.

52 See B. Cooper, *Beyond Respectability*.

53 Grosz, *Volatile Bodies*; Puar, "Cyborg," 63.

54 Crenshaw, "Demarginalizing," 149.

55 Puar, *Terrorist Assemblages*, 211–16.

56 Puar, "Cyborg," 53.

57 In *Habeas Viscus*, Alexander G. Weheliye turns to the racial assemblage as a way to discuss the work of Hortense Spillers and Sylvia Wynter, two Black women theorizing about Blackness and gender since "the idea of racializing assemblages ... construes race not as a biological or cultural classification but as a set of sociopolitical processes that discipline humanity into full humans, not-quite humans, and non-humans." He sets up these ideas in contrast to bare life (Agamben) and biopolitics (Foucault), which in their original instantiations ignore race and racism and their profound impact on notions of humanity. In as much as I find Weheliye's formulation useful, the assemblage, since it does not deal with biology or culture stringently, cannot account for the interplay between Blackness and madness in the same way as intersectionality does.

58 Cooper's project makes very clear that Black women's intellectual commitments were not incidental or coincidental. They were part of an intellectual tradition that theorized out of their quotidian embodied experience as a bulwark against racist and sexist material conditions. See B. Cooper, *Beyond Respectability*.

59 See B. Cooper, "Love No Limit."

60 Rosi Braidotti's text *The Posthuman* usefully explicates the intellectual lineage of the cyborg, noting that it comes from a set of ideas that privilege privileged conceptions of the human.

61 Siebers, *Disability Theory*; Kafer, *Feminist. Queer. Crip.*

62 See Pickens, *New Body Politics*, 116–46.

63 Vargas and James, "Refusing Blackness-as-Victimization," 198.

CONVERSATION 1. MAKING BLACK MADNESS

1 Bell, "Introducing White Disability Studies," 278.

2 Though Christopher M. Bell's essay holds this distinction, and rightfully so, he was not the only person to discuss race and ethnicity. Others—Rosemarie Garland Thomson, Douglas Baynton, David Yuan, and G. Thomas Couser—had done so before him. His contention was, and I concur, that disability studies as a field had consistently participated in the erasure, silencing, or ignoring of the intersections between these categories. He was the first to suggest (by not suggesting) a set of methodologies, analytical strategies, and representational politics.

3 Bell, "Representational Detective Work," 3.

4 Douglas Baynton's work discusses this in detail. He examines historical narratives in which disability and race or disability and gender intersect at the moment of articulating a claim to civil rights. See Baynton, "Disability and the Justification."

5 Cynthia Wu and Jennifer James ("Race, Ethnicity, Disability, and Literature") point this out in their introduction to *MELUS*'s special issue on race, ethnicity

and disability. Nirmala Erevelles, *Disability and Difference*, takes this topic up in her book-length study.

6 Samuels, *Fantasies of Identification*, 16.

7 Samuels, *Fantasies of Identification*, 9.

8 Octavia E. Butler bequeathed her archive to the Huntington Library, Art Collections, and Botanical Gardens in San Marino, California. The extensive collection spans approximately eight thousand folders and over three hundred boxes. It includes manuscripts, correspondence, journals, commonplace books, and ephemera.

9 In other work, I read Octavia E. Butler's *Fledgling* for how she theorizes Blackness and madness. This work was completed before I visited her archive at the Huntington Library, so it misses some of her theorizing. Also, the shorter article was designed to think through where and how the text dovetails with critical literature. This reading investigates how Butler's work shifts the critical terrain. See Pickens, "You're Supposed to Be."

10 Samuels, *Fantasies of Identification*, 11.

11 Samuels, *Fantasies of Identification*, 11.

12 Sander Gilman provides this historical context for his reading of the Black madman in Mark Twain's *Huckleberry Finn*. Gilman's reading, which appears verbatim in *Difference and Pathology* (137–40) and *On Blackness without Blacks* (6–8), grants some historical context to the discourses about Blackness and madness as they appear in the US public sphere.

13 Kim Nielsen's (*Disability History*) text works as an apt companion to those of Allison Carey and Nirmala Erevelles, who point out that the perception of mental illness is enough to warrant a conceptual and, at times, literal loss of citizenship rights. Nielsen's work establishes that link was made early in American history as a matter of defining citizenship.

14 Steven Noll and James Trent, Jr. (*Mental Retardation in America*, 1–19) clarify how the public discourse about mental illness undergoes slight shifts.

15 Jarman, "Dismembering the Lynch Mob," 91.

16 The phrase "turned out" has a slang meaning that refers to one's intensification of sexual desire in unexpected ways sometimes after having a (usually queer) sexual experience. Without carrying forward the homophobic connotations and logics, I do wish to harness the valences of the phrase that speak to various significant changes and shifts.

17 Holland, *Erotic Life of Racism*, 10.

18 Marlo David delineates how this functions in the category of neosoul music, particularly Erykah Badu's work, which draws heavily on these notions. Within this conversation, Mark Anthony Neal, Kodwo Eshun, Alondra Nelson, and Alexander Weheliye all trouble the idea that Blacks comfortably inhabit Western notions of time and progress. They each point out that Black cultural production muddies the understanding of Western time and space since it asserts the Black subject as a viable position. I discuss the import of this to humanist discourse in the third

conversation. See David, "Afrofuturism'" Neal, *Soul Babies*; Eshun, *More Brilliant than the Sun*; Nelson, "Introduction"; and Weheliye, "Feenin.'"

19 Bell, "Representational Detective Work," 3–4.

20 In another project, I discuss the way grammar determines responses to and about Black women's anger. This is another kind of madness, but the logic of dismissal tends to remain as part of the linguistic structures to which we have become accustomed in discussion. See Pickens, "The Verb Is No."

21 Michelle Jarman's work on Bebe Moore Campbell follows this logic. See Jarman, "Coming Up from Underground."

22 In another article (Pickens, "Modern Family"), I discuss Blackness as a "set of traditions, reading practices, and valuation systems operating alongside, intertwined with, but also independent from whiteness." My claims there sought to consider Blackness a paradigm from which to draw that does not operate in service of whiteness either to compare or castigate. Here I echo these claims.

23 Given the fact that disability studies (as a field) has tended to give primacy to physical disability, I am hesitant to collapse mental and physical disability. See Bérubé, *The Secret Life of Stories*; and Price, *Mad at School*. My aim here is to point out how much they are linked in this particular cultural context such that an analysis of one has repercussions for an analysis of the other. The two are decidedly not the same.

24 Thomson, *Extraordinary Bodies*, 103.

25 Thomson, *Extraordinary Bodies*, 106.

26 Thomson, *Extraordinary Bodies*, 104.

27 Thomson, *Extraordinary Bodies*, 105.

28 The difficulties of the social model of disability, particularly as it relates to mental illness and psychosocial disabilities, constitutes a larger conversation in disability studies. Scholars have come to understand that thinking in terms of the social model delimits our discussion of mental disability (broadly speaking) because it does not address how disability studies as a field relies on sanist conceptions of mind. For a brief and adroit discussion of these concerns, see Price, "Her Pronouns Wax and Wane."

29 Mrs. Hedges's understanding of her own relationship with Junto is figured not just through her own imagination but also through those of other characters. At several points in the novel, Mrs. Hedges's nebulous feelings for Junto and his seemingly unrequited feelings for her rise to the surface as a point of interest or contention. See Petry, *Street*, 247, 251, 275, 417.

30 "Misfits" is from Thomson, "Misfits."

31 Erevelles, "Color of Violence," 119.

32 Holland, *Erotic Life of Racism*, 7.

33 Holland, *Erotic Life of Racism*, 7, 20.

34 Jared Sexton takes up this line of argument in *Amalgamation Schemes* when discussing the way interracial sex tends to be viewed in limited terms—either naïve or bawdy—neither of which allow for the possibility of the messiness of sexual

relationships and which can also abet anti-Blackness at the center of multiracial discourse.

35 Other scholars have written about this extensively, focusing on the difficult choices her characters have to make because of these intimate relationships. See Govan, "Connections"; and Hampton, *Changing Bodies*.

36 Timothy S. Lyle used this phrase during a public conversation with Janet Mock, to describe Mock's (and others') decision to publicly open up the space for others. His idea speaks to the desire to expand how we think through a concept in the public realm. See Mock, "#RedefiningRealness."

37 Pickens, "You're Supposed to Be," 39.

38 Octavia E. Butler to Warner Books, 2005, Box 216, Octavia E. Butler Papers. Conventionally, one might attribute a "sic" to some of Butler's writing because it does not conform to standard English. Rather than label her bodymind a mistake or call attention to her writing as such (that is, embed ableism in my citational praxis and scholarship), I prefer to render the writing as is and ask people to engage with her grammar, spelling, and writing as a part of her theorizing.

39 Octavia E. Butler, journal, 2005, Box 60, Octavia E. Butler Papers.

40 Pickens, "You're Supposed to Be," 40.

41 Ellen Samuels ("My Body, My Closet") calls this a "coming out discourse," usually demanded of people with invisible disabilities.

42 Butler, *Fledgling*, 194.

43 I riff on W. E. B. Du Bois's notion of being a problem here because its understanding of two-ness is evocative in the consideration of Black madness and mad Blackness, keeping in mind that Du Bois's notion relies on Anna Julia Cooper's work in *A Voice from the South*. I also find it useful to point out that the one being considered the problem, in this instance, is not the one required to be clear about their status. It is those who consider Shori a problem who must—for their own sake as well—be aware of how her Black madness functions as a disruption of their social and cultural institutions.

44 Butler, *Fledgling*, 196.

45 Butler, *Fledgling*, 152, 266, 194.

46 Octavia E. Butler, journal, 2004, Box 39, Octavia E. Butler Papers.

47 Octavia E. Butler, journal, 2004, Box 39, Octavia E. Butler Papers.

48 Butler, *Fledgling*, 219; ellipses present in text.

49 This appears in several manuscript, correspondence, and journal boxes in the Octavia E. Butler Papers. She writes it as part of her notes to herself (Boxes 37–43, Box 169–72, Boxes 186–87), marginalia on letters from her editors (Boxes 215, 256), drafts of letters to her editors (Boxes 186–87), and in final versions of letters to her editors (Boxes 215, 256).

50 Octavia E. Butler to Seven Stories Press, 2005, Box 215, Octavia E. Butler Papers.

51 In thinking about the way Butler theorizes Daniel and Shori as a couple, it becomes important to consider how Shori embraces coevality rather than the

legitimizing nature of couplehood. Certainly, there is no guarantee that mating with Daniel would allow her to be considered fully Ina by her antagonists, but becoming part of a couple would legitimize her standing in Ina social and cultural terms—even if it is viewed as gauche. The decision to embrace coevality allows Shori to do some self-determination even if it is circumscribed by temporal parameters. This brief reading is inspired by Michael Cobb's work, *Single*.

52 Octavia E. Butler, commonplace books, 2005, Box 187, Octavia E. Butler Papers.

53 This fascination appears as early as 1974, though it may have occurred earlier given that symbiosis makes it way into drafts of *Kindred*, which she began conceptualizing in 1960. See Octavia E. Butler, journal, 1974, Box 56, Octavia E. Butler Papers.

54 Susana Morris ("Black Girls") discusses Wright's attraction and revulsion as well.

55 Octavia E. Butler, draft of *Asylum*, 2005, Box 8, Folder 79, Octavia E. Butler Papers.

56 Butler, *Fledgling*, 85.

57 Butler, *Fledgling*, 85–86.

58 This dovetails somewhat with a narrative that prematurely sexualizes Black girls. It is noteworthy because of Shori's appearance, since that has implications for Wright and other humans' interpretations of her. However, I have opted not to explore this interpretation because Shori is not a Black girl in terms of culture and age and does not understand herself that way. At this point in the text, the narrative does not present her as such. She is fifty-three, and, though still young for an Ina, she is not a child.

59 B. Smith, "Toward a Black Feminist Criticism," 164.

60 Monstrous intimacies are "defined as a set of known and unknown performances and inhabited horrors, desires and positions produced, reproduced, circulated, and transmitted, that are breathed in like air and often unacknowledged to be monstrous." See Sharpe, *Monstrous Intimacies*, 3.

61 Pickens, "Octavia Butler," 174–75.

62 Octavia E. Butler to Seven Stories Press, 2005, Box 215, Octavia E. Butler Papers.

63 Octavia E. Butler, draft of *Fledgling*, 2005, Box 37, Folder 599, Octavia E. Butler Papers.

64 Octavia E. Butler, draft of *Fledgling*, 2005, Box 38, Folders 649–50, Octavia E. Butler Papers.

65 Butler, *Fledgling*, 148.

66 Butler, *Fledgling*, 148.

67 Octavia E. Butler, draft of *Fledgling*, 2005, Box 39, Octavia E. Butler Papers.

68 Weheliye, *Habeas Viscus*.

69 Octavia E. Butler, draft of *Fledgling*, 2005, Box 40, Folder 704, Octavia E. Butler Papers.

70 Kafer, *Feminist. Queer. Crip.*, 2–3.

1 I deploy "thang" not only as a way to sonically signify on Black vernacular speech but also to evoke Aimé Césaire's concept of the "thingification" of Black people. My question is meant to ask about Black cultural contexts that affirm the validity of Blackness but also carry within them the potential to invalidate certain permutations of Black identity.

2 Davis, *Bending Over Backwards*, 147.

3 I have chosen not to explicitly treat anger here as part of the way madness works. For a discussion about Black anger, see Pickens, "The Verb Is No."

4 In an interview, Hopkinson clarifies that her interests and influences are wide-ranging. Though my project examines Black speculative fiction in particular, these artists-theorists' work should not be understood as exclusive to that category. See Nelson, "Making the Impossible Possible."

5 Titchkosky, *Reading and Writing Disability Differently*, 77.

6 Elam, "August Wilson," 612.

7 Harry Elam Jr. ("August Wilson") is not the only scholar to make use of this formulation. Michelle Elam (*Souls of Mixed Folks*) takes up this concept to describe the way mixed race protagonists in anti-*bildungsromane* resist their incorporation into racial logics of ontology. Nicole Fleetwood ("Case of Rihanna") pinpoints how these logics work in her discussion of the public reception of pop star Rihanna. La Marr Bruce ("The People Inside My Head, Too") finds similar logics at work in the public reception of Lauryn Hill.

8 It is useful to note that sociogenic madness corresponds to an understanding of madness as communally determined, but by a community to which the so-called mad person does not necessarily belong. Jonathan Metzl's (*Protest Psychosis*) work examines this phenomenon more thoroughly. He suggests that mental illness and diagnosis thereof for Black folks, particularly in the twentieth century, cannot be detached from a sociogenic element.

9 Bérubé's *Secret Life of Stories* hinges on the apt provocation that we consider how the novel form demands a kind of illegibility vis-à-vis cognition and (somewhat) forecloses this possibility of representation. In that way, all texts are in some way about specific modes of cognition. There is a new volume that explores the lives of people of color living with autism. See Brown, Ashkenazy, and Onaiwu, *All the Weight*.

10 Boster, "Unfit for Ordinary Purposes," 203

11 Lawrie, "Salvaging the Negro," 323

12 Rosemarie Garland Thomson (*Staring*) describes the stare as a question and an interrogation that forces a kind of visibility and foists a set of expectations on the disabled.

13 In Black vernacular, "feature" means to exhibit in a particularly cinematic fashion. It means to center someone's thoughts or ideas, to study them and take them seriously. The term also functions as a critique of the way someone who is

not featured is not entertained in thought and not entertaining or pleasurable to think about.

14 As Catherine Prendergast ("On the Rhetorics of Mental Disability") points out, "To be disabled mentally is to be disabled rhetorically." The two accompany each other as narratives about mental disability and about rhetorical possibility.

15 Hopkinson, "Interview with Nalo Hopkinson," 149

16 Hopkinson, "Interview with Nalo Hopkinson," 150.

17 Here, I pull from ideas in Kevin Quashie's *The Sovereignty of Quiet* and Darlene Clark Hine's idea of cultures of dissemblance in "Rape and the Inner Lives of Black Women in the Middle West."

18 Titchkosky, *Reading and Writing Disability*, 115.

19 Murray, *Representing Autism*, 19.

20 Murray, *Representing Autism*, 20.

21 Yergeau, "Clinically Significant Disturbance."

22 Chew, "Disabled Speech."

23 E. Smith, *Globalization*, 52. Please note the use of "on Toussaint" rather than "in Toussaint." Since Toussaint is another planet, I use the preposition "on" to communicate the location as such. This also corresponds with the use of "on" in Black vernacular speech i.e., "on today" as a way of signifying on and indexing time and space as nuanced or emphasized ideological spaces.

24 Here, I am thinking mostly of narratives about autistics in which the autistic person does not participate in controlling or shaping the narrative as much as the parent, so-called advocate, or medical professional. See Jack; Murray, *Representing Autism*; and Yergeau ("Clinically Significant Disturbance").

25 Hopkinson, *Midnight Robber*, 73.

26 Hopkinson, *Midnight Robber*, 73.

27 Nirmala Erevelles makes this point in much of her work, clarifying that the sacrosanct rules of ignoring the origins of impairment do not work when discussing how impairment occurs in racialized, globalized spaces.

28 Hopkinson, *Midnight Robber*, 129.

29 Hopkinson, *Midnight Robber*, 129.

30 I make this point more forcefully when discussing a critical turn to Blackness. See Pickens, "Modern Family."

31 Chen, *Animacies*, 43.

32 Chen, *Animacies*, 42.

33 Hopkinson, *Midnight Robber*, 128–29.

34 Chen, *Animacies*, 127.

35 For those tempted to read Quamina's disappearance as evidence of narrative asymmetry vis-à-vis disability, it is worth noting that she disappears from narrative view for reasons related to the plotline. Her disappearance is not contingent on an ableist narrative of erasure or the plotline's prioritizing of Tan-Tan's disability over hers.

36 See Boyle, "Vanishing Bodies"; and Braithwaite, "Connecting to a Future Community."

37 Part of the problem with considering this the ending or a reconciliation is that it assumes that Tan-Tan's public telling allows her to snap out of the mental illness induced by her trauma. As Andrea Nicki ("Abused Mind," 81) writes, "Social structures [of which literary criticism is one] based on able-mindedness, which marginalize people with mental illnesses, and assume that they can simply 'snap out' of their conditions, are also disabling." Another concern is that the sanist mapping dovetails with a set of ideas that erase madness according to sanist privilege. For the ways that this functions, see Wolframe, "Madwoman in the Academy."

38 Nicki, "Abused Mind," 81.

39 Hopkinson, *Midnight Robber*, 320.

40 Hopkinson, *Midnight Robber*, 323.

41 In thinking about the multiple analyses the community has, it becomes imperative to contemplate how much of those are related to their desires to police the community and also the availability of their pleasure. For more on how this works vis-à-vis disability (particularly invisible and stigmatized disability) in Black communities, see Lyle, "Trying to Scrub."

42 Hopkinson, *Midnight Robber*, 324.

43 Hopkinson, *Midnight Robber*, 325.

44 Hopkinson, *Midnight Robber*, 325.

45 Hopkinson, *Midnight Robber*, 190–92, 220–30, 246, 255, 309.

46 Hopkinson, *Midnight Robber*, 51.

47 Hopkinson, *Midnight Robber*, 51.

48 Alexander Weheliye ("Feenin'") and Marlo David ("Afrofuturism") point out that Black sonics trouble the traditional idea of the posthuman. They each explore how contemporary Black music shifts the understandings of technology and culture.

49 Lennard Davis describes reading as an act that does not usually require speaking or hearing, calling it a deafened moment. See Davis, *Enforcing Normalcy*.

50 Hopkinson, *Midnight Robber*, 1.

51 Boyle, "Vanishing Bodies," 181.

52 E. Smith, *Globalization*, 43.

53 E. Smith, *Globalization*, 55.

54 See Enteen, "On the Receiving End."

55 Braithwaite, "Connecting to a Future Community," 83.

56 In the spirit of conversation, I turn to a meditation on Granny Nanny as a cyborg. Partially historical figure, partially created technosavvy system—she does fit the bill in a, forgive me, technical sense. She also foregrounds many of the concerns I wrote regarding the blasphemy of the cyborg figure as it relates to anti-Blackness and ableism. The power Granny Nanny solidifies corresponds to a set of realities that eschews working-class material realities: no one on Toussaint performs manual labor, and those that do refuse to be a part of the Granny Nanny system completely. Their decision to opt in ostensibly rests on their desire for privacy, but it also permits them to escape the surveillance and power

Granny Nanny imposes and represents. Moreover, Granny Nanny's theodicy makes her ethically suspicious vis-à-vis the population she oversees. For whom does she solidify her power through Tan-Tan and Tan-Tan's child? If it is for the Marryshow Corporation, Granny Nanny's allegiance to corporate power is not just about capitalist greed but also functions as a betrayal of the historical figure upon which she is based. The freedom fighter who would use her genitals in warfare—the so-called real Granny Nanny—no longer applies here; instead, this Granny Nanny works to foreclose agentive possibility. Similar to Vargas and James's ("Refusing Blackness-as-Victimization") forgiving cyborg (who abets anti-Blackness by requiring Black self-abnegation), Granny Nanny's quest for power and usurpation of human agency overshadows the potential political possibilities of community and coalition building (however fraught they are). Herein lies the problem with the cyborg paradigm. In thinking about Granny Nanny as a cyborg, we find some utility in her blasphemy as a corporate shill, complexity in her vexed relationship to human agency, and tension in understanding her as a mélange of historical and futuristic figures. Nonetheless, each instantiation leads us back to the anxiety of the missing Black human, since they are all predicated on an erasure of Blackness. In the case of capitalist allegiance, that Blackness is material. In the case of human agency, that Blackness is cultural. In the case of historical and futuristic figures, that Blackness is social and historical. These versions of Granny Nanny also assume a particular kind of mind, even as Granny Nanny attempts to control that mind. Here, not only does the cyborg erase the Black human but that erasure is predicated on a sanist conception of the Black human as unable to perform the cognitive function required to exist on its own terms. Thinking through Granny Nanny as a cyborg demonstrates what Alison Kafer (*Feminist. Queer. Crip.*) speculates is true: that the cyborg paradigm may not be useful at all. That is, even as this thought experiment raises interesting questions, those questions and the answers usher in ethically suspicious ideas wedded to anti-Blackness and sanism.

57 Weheliye, *Habeas Viscus*, 19.

CONVERSATION 3. ABANDONING THE HUMAN?

1 Thomson, *Extraordinary Bodies*, 8.
2 Alison Kafer and Erica Edwards discuss this method as a way of participating in an endless questioning of the premises and resulting conclusions of our analyses. See Kafer, *Feminist.Queer.Crip.*; and Edwards, *Charisma*.
3 Scholars familiar with the discussion of the human may wonder why I choose not to engage thinkers in posthumanism more explicitly. In consonance with the aim of this text to open up the conversation within Black studies and disability studies, I choose to focus on the discussions about the human that use disability or Blackness as their central focus and starting point. This shifts the locus of the conversation from being mostly located in or on Enlightenment traditions, recasting the conversation so that it begins with Blackness and/or

madness at the center. This movement away from posthumanism also surfaces in my rationale for not mobilizing the cyborg and cyborgian theory for these discussions.

4 See Wynter, "Africa."

5 This particular strand of thought runs through the majority of Wynter's oeuvre. In this moment, I refer to "Unsettling the Coloniality."

6 I do not simply mean the link between Blackness and premature death, though that link has been clearly established. I also refer to the philosophical theodicy question of who gets to count as human. The two are intimately related. See Gordon, "Race."

7 See Moten, "Blackness and Nothingness."

8 In placing these two side by side, I do not collapse their arguments, especially since Sexton takes issue with Moten in the article cited here. On one aspect of Blackness (at least) they are in agreement: abjection and degradation remain a part of Black experiences the world over. See Sexton, "Social Life of Social Death."

9 Each of the scholars mentioned here has a monograph (or two) that discusses how the antebellum period reaches into the present moment. Their Black feminist research spans from art to literature to philosophy, but each begins from the same premise: that the Middle Passage and the antebellum period cannot be ignored as current influences on Black life. See Brown, *Repeating Body*; Hartman, *Scenes of Subjection* and *Lose Your Mother*; Sharpe, *Monstrous Intimacies* and *In the Wake*; Spillers, *Black, White, and in Color*, and Weheliye, *Habeas Viscus*.

10 Here, I reference the work of Frank B. Wilderson, Sharon P. Holland, and Darieck Scott, each of whom examines the vexed spaces where Blackness is considered abjection, but where Black strategies of resistance also surface. In each of these cases, Blackness reckons with abjection by attempting to mobilize it—grammatically, erotically, theoretically—toward the end of what Fred Moten might term an unfree freedom.

11 I have deliberately chosen Michael Jackson's lyric as a way to describe this positionality. His role in *The Wiz*, as the scarecrow, without a brain, foregrounds the interrelatedness of madness, Blackness, and personhood. Within the Black production, disability remains a penumbral presence. It is my contention that one cannot wrestle with race without examining the itinerant ableist narratives that accompany it. I make this point within the text. See endnote 20 that follows, and M. Jackson, "You Can't Win."

12 This point surfaces in the debate between Peter Singer and Harriet McBryde Johnson. See Johnson, "Should I Have Been Killed?"

13 Sontag, *Illness as Metaphor*.

14 I have always found Lennard Davis's point regarding Venus de Milo very provocative. It reminds us how much the presence of disability pervades our experience but is often not acknowledged as disability. See Davis, *Enforcing Normalcy*.

15 Davidson, "Aesthetics."

16 Christopher M. Bell makes this point in several of his articles. Inasmuch as it is

present in the most often cited article, "Introducing White Disability Studies," and in the introduction to his edited volume *Blackness and Disability*, "Doing Representational Detective Work," he argues this point about Earvin "Magic" Johnson in another article. Bell makes the point that by erasure and the use of coded language, people of color find ways to discuss disability without discussing it outright and in so doing create narratives about disability that are shaped and shaping the discursive terrain. Michael Bérubé makes this same point about intellectual disability in his monograph *The Secret Life of Stories*. See Bell, "Problem with Magic"; and Bérubé, *Secret Life of Stories*.

17 Within the fields of rhetoric and communication, Jay Dolmage and Stephanie Kerschbaum have each intervened in commonly held notions about how disability functions in discursive space. Dolmage makes the case that long-standing histories in rhetoric require disabled bodies to make themselves legible, usually according to ableist scripts. Kerschbaum critiques the way disability gets coopted as a matter of selling diversity and/or making it more palatable for those who consider it abject. See Dolmage, *Disability Rhetoric*; and Kerschbaum, *Toward a New Rhetoric of Difference*.

18 Siebers, *Disability Theory*, 1–34.

19 McRuer, *Crip Theory*, 207.

20 I have deliberately chosen Michael Jackson's lyric as a way to describe this positionality. As a sonic reference, *Thriller* marks Jackson's transition from being a United States-based pop star to a global pop icon because of its sales. The collaboration with Quincy Jones, famed for his production style based on Black music forms, also marks that transition as beholden to Blackness. I use it here to describe disability because I question the possibility of universality without a reckoning with Blackness. As a figure, Jackson functions at shorthand for this critique since I do wanna be starting something, which I elaborate in the text. I also make a similar critique earlier in the text. See previous footnote (#11) and M. Jackson, "Wanna Be Startin' Something."

21 Siebers, *Disability Theory*, 48.

22 Snyder and Mitchell, *Cultural Locations of Disability*, 127–28.

23 Siebers, *Disability Theory*, 5.

24 Bruce, "Mad Is a Place," 304.

25 I refer to two scholars in particular. Tobin Siebers's work in *Disability Theory* requests that scholars acknowledge and discuss what he terms the negative aspects of disability, though he hints that negative feelings about disability evince an investment in the ideology of ability. Alison Kafer provides an apt reading of the limitations of disability futurity in *Feminist.Queer.Crip.* wherein she pinpoints the difficulty with embracing disability as a disabled person.

26 Multiple scholars who work on madness take disability studies to task for ignoring cognitive disability and mental illness. This critique is most forceful in Catherine Prendergast's "On the Rhetorics of Mental Disability."

27 This should not be confused with a nonhuman turn. My aim is not to decenter the human in favor of an engagement with the nonhuman but rather to ques-

tion the way we understand the human as a valid category. For a discussion of the nonhuman turn as such, see Grusin.

28 Though Prince was not the first person to invoke this idea, I would be remiss if I did not acknowledge that he as an artist-theorist experiments with Black cultural and musical notions of what it means to be Black forever, love Blackness forever.

29 Bérubé, *Secret Life of Stories*, 4.

30 Though Walcott discusses Canada in his article specifically, part of his argumentative thrust requires a look at the way cultural production operates in the United States as well. His point in acceding to the warnings of Stuart Hall is that Canada's interaction with the Black population therein—through erasure and institutional racism—is not unique, particularly in the way it surfaces in pop culture. See Walcott, "Caribbean Pop Culture in Canada."

31 Jonas's book *The Battle of Adwa* treats the latter part of the nineteenth century and its aftermath. Though in the introduction Jonas titillates the readers with the idea that "history loves exceptions," the rest of the account suggests that Adwa was not as exceptional as Jonas might have thought. In fact, the Ethiopians defeated the Italians in several battles before October 1896. Though labeling Adwa an exception implies the impossibility of duplication, or that it was a fluke, the strategy on the part of Menelik and Taytu gives the lie to that idea.

32 This appears multiple times over Due's *Blood Colony* (91 and 209) and *My Soul to Take* (248).

33 Donadey, "Postslavery and Postcolonial Representations," 76.

34 Sharon P. Holland draws this out further in her discussion of racism as a project of belonging in her *Erotic Life of Racism*.

35 Due, *Living Blood*, 489.

36 Due, *Living Blood*, 488.

37 Simplican, *Capacity Contract*, 119.

38 Due, *Blood Colony*, 75, 78.

39 Due, *Blood Colony*, 404, 213.

40 Bell, "Doing Representational Detective Work," 1–2.

41 Hartman, *Scenes of Subjection*, 19.

42 Due, *My Soul to Take*, 335.

43 Due, *My Soul to Take*, 335–36.

44 Paris is indeed burning, hunties. See *Paris*.

45 I invoke Shakespeare here for several reasons: First, I want to point to the hegemony of whiteness in our understanding of the literary canon. Second, I understand this sonnet's questioning of "what's in a name?" to be an apt way to point out the futility of describing Charlie/Michel as mixed race as an attempt to erase his whiteness and his preference for white supremacy. Third, puns and witticisms are part of my personal writing style. It is what the British might term cheeky.

46 Due, *My Soul to Take*, 106.

1 Wright, *Physics of Blackness*; emphasis in original.

2 Eyre, "Deafened by Laughter," 31.

3 This is not a discussion of the novel form in a structuralist sense. I am not interested in thinking about the novel's construction. Instead, I am more concerned with the novel as an ideological project, perhaps a Black, mad project, in a mad Black tradition.

4 In the introduction to *Speculative Blackness*, carrington describes his project as having a broader reach because of the way popular culture and literature function together.

5 This is not meant to be an offhand statement that endorses the novel as a utopian space. Instead, I draw from multiple scholars who work on Blackness and disability, who suggest that the novel offers a complex space to render these identities, one whose possibilities of representation create a certain kind of safety to explore. I point to Catherine Prendergast's ("Race") analysis of Derrick Bell in which she discusses the difficulty people had when interpreting his fiction because it neither ratified conservative ideology nor exploited Black pathos. Percival Everett's work in *Erasure* is a fictionalized account of this same idea. Gene Jarrett makes a similar claim in *Representing the Race* when he discusses the import of literature to discussions of informal politics for Black authors and audiences.

6 Popp, "Eloquent Limbs," 39.

7 See Bérubé, "Disability and Narrative"; Schalk, "Interpreting Disability Metaphor and Race"; and Tyler, "Jim Crow's Disabilities."

8 Mitchell and Snyder, *Narrative Prosthesis*.

9 Titchkosky, *Reading and Writing Disability Differently*, 7.

10 Those familiar with Johnson's work will know that he relies on Faustian bargains for *Hunting in Harlem* and *Papa Midnite*. He also relies on monsters in *Papa Midnite* and *Pym*.

11 Felman, "Writing and Madness," 18.

12 Yergeau, "Aut(hored)ism."

13 M. Johnson, "Foreword."

14 M. Johnson, "Foreword."

15 M. Johnson, "Foreword."

16 In some ways, I want this to shadow the text in the same way that the link between Blackness and sexual deviance functions in my discussion of Octavia E. Butler's theorizing in *Fledgling* (see conversation 1) with all that this entails in terms of difficulty dealing with a Blackness and a madness that refuses to be disciplined by white able-bodied masculinity.

17 Scott, *Extravagant Abjection*, 5; emphasis in original.

18 Without tracing this strain through the entirety of the black novel tradition, it becomes imperative to examine scholarship that has done so. There are quite a

few that are too numerous to name here. A few in particular inspire this discussion because of their recent publication. See Jarrett, *Deans and Truants*; Jarrett, *Representing the Race*; Jenkins, *Private Lives, Proper Relations;* Sharpe, *Monstrous Intimacies*; Abdur-Rahman, *Against the Closet*; and Scott, *Extravagant Abjection.*

19 Sharpe, *In the Wake*, 4; emphasis in original.

20 This statement inspired by Michelle Elam in *The Souls of Mixed Folk.*

21 M. Johnson, *Hunting in Harlem*, 1.

22 I'm deliberately making a distinction here between recidivism and abjection because there are significant institutional and structural challenges that help to create recidivism. The position itself is not abject, though it tends to be deeply imbricated with notions and circumstances of abjection. See Alexander, *New Jim Crow*; and Travis, *But They All Come Back.*

23 This does not endorse or argue for thinking of Bobby as a figure that overcomes his criminality, skeptical as I am about the critical payoff and accuracy of such a reading from both a disability studies and Black studies perspective. Instead, I read Bobby as a character that must deploy his pyromania in service of his desire to become writer, rather than a killer.

24 Felman, "Writing and Madness," 50.

25 M. Johnson, *Hunting in Harlem*, 168.

26 M. Johnson, *Hunting in Harlem*, 168.

27 M. Johnson, *Hunting in Harlem*, 168.

28 M. Johnson, *Hunting in Harlem*, 167.

29 One of the concerns in interpreting Bobby's novel would be its engagement with the environment. Camille T. Dungy's edited volume *Black Nature*, though it anthologizes poetry, explains why a reading public has been resistant to Black engagements with nature.

30 Norris, "Satire of John Killens," 186.

31 Bobby's commentary about the nonreaders of his novel suggests that he thinks they only want to read books that have little substance. Bobby extends this commentary to the readers of his competitor, Bo Shareef, who writes a book titled *Datz What I'm Talkin' 'Bout*, which Bobby terms unreadable trash.

32 Darryl Smith's work builds on this notion by asserting that irreverence is one of the ways that Black combative humor uses the malleability of a Black cultural context to reshape conversations about disability as redemptive. See D. Smith, "Handi-/Cappin' Slaves."

33 M. Johnson, *Hunting in Harlem*, 169.

34 M. Johnson, *Hunting in Harlem*, 170.

35 M. Johnson, *Hunting in Harlem*, 170.

36 M. Johnson, "Foreword."

37 See Jarrett, *Representing the Race.*

Abdur-Rahman, Aliyyah R. *Against the Closet: Black Political Longing and the Erotics of Race*. Durham, NC: Duke University Press, 2012.

Agamben, Giorgio. *Homo Sacer: Sovereign Power and Bare Life*. Translated by Daniel Heller-Roazen. Stanford, CA: Stanford University Press, 1998.

Aho, Tanja, Liat Ben-Moshe, and Leon J. Hilton. "Introduction: Mad Futures: Affect/Theory/Violence." *Mad Futures: Affect/Theory/Violence*. Edited by Tanja Aho, Liat Ben-Moshe, and Leon J. Hilton. Special issue, *American Quarterly* 69, no. 2 (2017): 291–303.

Alexander, Michelle. *The New Jim Crow*. New York: New Press, 2010.

Amin, Takiyah Nur. "Beyond Hierarchy: Reimagining African Diaspora Dance in Higher Education Curricula." *Black Scholar* 46, no. 1 (2016): 15–26.

Amin, Takiyah Nur. "A Scholar Tea with Dr. Takiyah Amin—Black Aesthetics: Culture, Performance and Scholarship." Public conversation, March 9, 2016, Commons 226, Bates College, Lewiston, ME.

Bailey, Moya. "'The Illest': Disability as Metaphor in Hip Hop Music." In *Blackness and Disability: Critical Examinations and Cultural Interventions*, edited by Christopher M. Bell, 141–48. East Lansing: Michigan State Press, 2011.

Barker, Claire. "Interdisciplinary Dialogues: Disability and Post-Colonial Studies." *Review of Disability Studies: An International Journal* 6, no. 8 (2010): 15–24.

Barr, Marleen S. "'All at One Point' Conveys the Point, Period: Or, Black Science Fiction Is Bursting Out All Over." In *Afro-Future Females: Black Writers Chart Science Fiction's Newest New-Wave Trajectory*, edited by Marleen S. Barr, ix–xxiv. Columbus: Ohio State University, 2008.

Baynton, Douglas. "Disability and the Justification of Inequality in American History." In *New Disability History*, edited by Paul Longmore and Lauri Umansky, 33–57. New York: New York University Press, 2001.

Bell, Christopher M., ed. *Blackness and Disability: Critical Examinations and Cultural Interventions*. East Lansing: Michigan State Press, 2011.

Bell, Christopher M. "Introducing White Disability Studies: A Modest Proposal." In *The Disability Studies Reader*, edited by Lennard Davis, 275–82. 2nd ed. New York: Routledge, 2006.

Bell, Christopher M. "The Problem with Magic in/and Representing AIDS." In *Culture and the State: Alternative Interventions*, edited by J. Gifford and G. Zezulka-Mailloux, 7–23. Vol. 4. Edmonton, AB: CRC Studio Publishers, 2003.

Bell, Christopher M. "Doing Representational Detective Work." In *Blackness and Disability: Critical Examinations and Cultural Interventions*, edited by Christopher M. Bell, 1–7. East Lansing: Michigan State Press, 2011.

Bérubé, Michael. "Disability and Narrative." *PMLA* 120, no. 2 (2005): 568–76.

Bérubé, Michael. *The Secret Life of Stories: From Don Quixote to Harry Potter: How Understanding Intellectual Disability Transforms the Way We Read*. New York: New York University Press, 2016.

Boster, Dea H. *African American Slavery and Disability*. New York: Routledge, 2013.

Boster, Dea H. "'Unfit for Ordinary Purposes': Disability, Slaves, and Decision Making in the Antebellum American South." In *Disability Histories*, edited by Susan Burch and Michael Rembis, 201–17. Urbana: University of Illinois Press, 2014.

Boyle, Elizabeth. "Vanishing Bodies: 'Race' and Technology in Nalo Hopkinson's *Midnight Robber*." *African Identities* 7, no. 2 (2009): 177–91.

Braidotti, Rosi. *The Posthuman*. Cambridge, UK: Polity Press, 2013.

Braithwaite, Alisa K. "Connecting to a Future Community: Storytelling, the Database, and Nalo Hopkinson's *Midnight Robber*." In *The Black Imagination: Science Fiction, Futurism, and the Speculative*, edited by Sandra Jackson and Julie E. Moody-Freeman, 81–99. New York: Peter Lang, 2011.

Brown, Kimberly Juanita. *The Repeating Body: Slavery's Visual Resonance in the Contemporary*. Durham, NC: Duke University Press, 2015.

Brown, Linda, E. Ashkenazy, and Morénike Giwa Onaiwu, eds. *All the Weight of Our Dreams: On Living Racialized Autism*. Lincoln, NE: DragonBee Press, 2017.

Bruce, La Marr Jurelle. "Mad Is a Place; or, the Slave Ship Tows the Ship of Fools." *Mad Futures: Affect/Theory/Violence*. Edited by Tanja Aho, Liat Ben-Moshe, and Leon J. Hilton. Special issue, *American Quarterly* 69, no. 2 (2017): 303–8.

Bruce, La Marr Jurelle. "'The People inside My Head, Too': Madness, Black Womanhood, and the Radical Performance of Lauryn Hill." *On Black Performance*. Edited by Soyica Colbert. Special issue, *African American Review* 45, no. 3 (2012): 371–89.

Brune, Jeffrey A. "Blind Like Me: John Howard Griffin, Disability, Intersectionality and Civil Rights in Post-Civil War America." *Blackness and Disability*. Edited by Therí A. Pickens. Special issue, *African American Review* 50, no. 2 (2017): 203–19.

Burch, Susan and Hannah Joyner. *Unspeakable: The Story of Junius Wilson*. Chapel Hill: University of North Carolina Press, 2007.

Butler, Octavia E. *Fledgling*. New York: Grand Central, 2007.

Butler, Octavia E., Papers. 1933–2006. Huntington Library, Art Collections, and Botanical Gardens, San Marino, CA.

Butler, Octavia E. "Positive Obsession." *Bloodchild and Other Stories*. New York: Seven Stories Press, 2005.

Calamur, Krishnadev. "Ferguson Documents: Officer Darren Wilson's Testimony." *National Public Radio*, November 25, 2014. https://www.npr.org/sections /thetwo-way/2014/11/25/366519644/ferguson-docs-officer-darren-wilsons -testimony.

Carey, Allison C. *On the Margins of Citizenship: Intellectual Disability and Civil Rights in Twentieth-Century America*. Philadelphia, PA: Temple University Press, 2009.

Carey, Tamika L. *Rhetorical Healing: The Reeducation of Contemporary Black Womanhood*. Albany, NY: SUNY Press, 2016.

carrington, andré m. *Speculative Blackness: The Future of Race in Science Fiction*. Minneapolis: University of Minnesota Press, 2016.

Cartwright, Samuel A. "Diseases and Peculiarities of the Negro Race." *De Bow's Review Southern and Western States*. Last modified January 30 2012, http://www .pbs.org/wgbh/aia/part4/4h3106t.html.

Césaire, Aimé. *Discourse on Colonialism*. Translated by Joan Pinkham. New York: Monthly Review Press, 2001.

Chen, Mel. *Animacies: Biopolitics, Racial Mattering, and Queer Affect*. Durham, NC: Duke University Press, 2012.

Cheng, Anne. *The Melancholy of Race: Psychoanalysis, Assimilation and Hidden Grief*. New York: Oxford University Press, 2001.

Chew, Kristina. "The Disabled Speech of Asian Americans: Silence and Autism in Lois-Ann Yamanaka's *Father of the Four Passages*." *Disability Studies Quarterly* 30, no. 1 (2010). www.dsq-sds.com.

Christian, Barbara. "The Race for Theory." In *African American Literary Theory*, edited by Winston Napier, 280–89. New York: New York University Press, 2000.

Cobb, Michael. *Single: Arguments for the Uncoupled*. New York: New York University Press, 2012.

Cohen, Cathy J. *The Boundaries of Blackness: AIDS and the Breakdown of Black Politics*. Chicago, IL: University of Chicago Press, 1999.

Coleman, Wanda. *Imagoes*. New York: Black Sparrow Press, 1983.

Cooper, Anna Julia. *A Voice from the South*. Xenia, OH: Aldine Printing House, 1892.

Cooper, Brittney. *Beyond Respectability: The Intellectual Thought of Race Women*. Champaign: University of Illinois Press, 2017.

Cooper, Brittney. "Love No Limit: Towards a Black Feminist Future (In Theory)." *Black Scholar* 45, no. 4 (2015): 7–21.

Couser, G. Thomas. *Recovering Bodies: Illness, Disability, and Life Writing*. Madison: University of Wisconsin Press, 1997.

Crenshaw, Kimberlé. "Demarginalizing the Intersection of Race and Sex: A Black

Feminist Critique of Antidiscrimination Doctrine, Feminist Theory and Anti-racist Politics." *The University of Chicago Legal Forum Volume 1989: Feminism in the Law: Theory, Practice, and Criticism* 140 (1989): 139–67.

Crenshaw, Kimberlé. "Mapping the Margins: Intersectionality, Identity Politics, and Violence against Women of Color." *Stanford Law Review* 6 (1991): 1241–99.

Cvetkovich, Ann. *Depression: A Public Feeling.* Durham, NC: Duke University Press, 2012.

Danquah, Meri Nana-Ama. *Willow Weep for Me: A Black Woman's Journey through Depression, A Memoir.* New York: Ballantine Books, 1998.

David, Marlo. "Afrofuturism and Post-Soul Possibility in Black Popular Culture." *African American Review* 41, no. 4 (2007): 695–707.

Davidson, Michael. "Aesthetics." In *Keywords for Disability Studies*, edited by Rachel Adams, Benjamin Reiss, and David Serlin, 30. New York: New York University Press, 2015.

Davis, Lennard J. *Bending Over Backwards: Disability, Dismodernism, and other Difficult Positions.* New York: New York University Press, 2002.

Davis, Lennard J. *The End of Normal: Identity in a Biocultural Era.* Ann Arbor: University of Michigan Press, 2014.

Davis, Lennard J. *Enforcing Normalcy: Disability, Deafness, and the Body.* New York: Verso, 1995.

Deleuze, Gilles. *The Fold: Leibniz and the Baroque.* Translated by Tom Conley. Minneapolis: University of Minnesota Press, 1992.

Dolmage, Jay. *Disability Rhetoric.* Syracuse, NY: Syracuse University Press, 2014.

Donadey, Anne. "Postslavery and Postcolonial Representations: Comparative Approaches." In *The Creolization of Theory*, edited by Françoise Lionnet and Shu-mei Shih, 62–82. Durham, NC: Duke University Press, 2011.

Donaldson, Elizabeth, and Catherine Prendergast. "There's No Crying in Disability Studies!" *Disability and Emotion.* Edited by Elizabeth Donaldson and Catherine Prendergast. Special issue, *Journal of Literary and Cultural Disability Studies* 5, no. 2 (2011): 129–36.

Du Bois, W. E. B. *The Souls of Black Folk.* Avenel, NJ: Gramercy Books, 1994.

Due, Tananarive. *Blood Colony.* New York: Washington Square Press, 2008.

Due, Tananarive. *The Living Blood.* New York: Washington Square Press, 2001.

Due, Tananarive. *My Soul to Keep.* New York: Eos, 1997.

Due, Tananarive. *My Soul to Take.* New York: Washington Square Press, 2011.

Dungy, Camille T., ed. *Black Nature: Four Centuries of African American Nature Poetry.* Athens: University of Georgia Press, 2009.

Edwards, Erica. *Charisma and the Fictions of Black Leadership.* Minneapolis: University of Minnesota Press, 2012.

Elam Jr., Harry J. "August Wilson, Doubling, Madness, and Modern African-American Drama." *Modern Drama* 43 (2000): 611–32.

Elam, Michelle. *The Souls of Mixed Folks: Race, Politics, and Aesthetics in the New Millennium.* Stanford, CA: Stanford University Press, 2011.

Enteen, Jillana. "'On the Receiving End of the Colonization': Nalo Hopkinson's 'Nansi Web." *Science Fiction Studies* 34 (2007): 262–82.

Erevelles, Nirmala. "Becoming Disabled / Becoming Black: Crippin' Critical Ethnic Studies from the Periphery." In *Critical Ethnic Studies: A Reader*, edited by Critical Ethnic Studies Editorial Collective, 231–51. Durham, NC: Duke University Press, 2016

Erevelles, Nirmala. "The Color of Violence: Reflecting on Gender, Race, and Disability in Wartime." In *Feminist Disability Studies*, edited by Kim Q. Hall, 117–35. Bloomington: Indiana University Press, 2011.

Erevelles, Nirmala. "Crippin' Jim Crow: Disability, Dis-Location, and the School-to-Prison Pipeline." In *Disability Incarcerated: Imprisonment and Disability in the United States and Canada*, edited by Liat Ben-Moshe, Chris Chapman, and Allison C. Carey, 81–100. New York: Palgrave McMillan, 2014.

Erevelles, Nirmala. *Disability and Difference in Global Contexts: Enabling a Transformative Body Politic.* New York: Palgrave McMillan, 2012.

Eshun, Kodwo. *More Brilliant Than the Sun: Adventures in Sonic Fiction.* London, UK: Quartet Books, 1998.

Everett, Percival. *Erasure.* New York: Graywolf Press, 2011.

Eyre, Pauline. "Deafened by Laughter: Reading David Lodge's *Deaf Sentences* as a Carnivalesque Embodiment." *Journal of Literary & Cultural Disability Studies* 6, no. 1 (2017): 17–34.

Fadda, Carol. Review of *New Body Politics: Narrating Arab and Black Identity in the Contemporary United States* by Therí A. Pickens. *Mashriq & Mahjar* 2, no. 2 (2014): 152–54.

Felman, Shoshana. "Writing and Madness: From Henry James: Writing and the Risks of Practice (Turning the Screw of Interpretation)." In *The Claims of Literature: A Shoshana Felman Reader*, edited by Emily Sun, Eyal Peretz, and Ulrich Baer, 15–50. New York: Fordham University Press, 2007.

Felman, Shoshana. *Writing and Madness: Literature/Philosophy/Psychoanalysis.* Translated by Martha Noel Evans. Palo Alto, CA: Stanford University Press, 2003.

Finney, Nikky. *Head Off & Split.* Evanston, IL: TriQuarterly Books / Northwestern University Press, 2011.

Fleetwood, Nicole. "The Case of Rihanna: Erotic Violence and Black Female Desire." *On Black Performance.* Edited by Soyica Colbert. Special issue, *African American Review* 45, no. 3 (2012): 419–35.

Gates Jr., Henry Louis. *The Signifying Monkey: A Theory of African American Literary Criticism.* New York: Oxford University Press, 1988.

Gill, Michael, and Nirmala Erevelles. "The Absent Presence of Elsie Lacks: Hauntings at the Intersection of Race, Class, Gender, and Disability." *Blackness and Disability.* Edited by Therí A. Pickens. Special issue, *African American Review*, 50, no. 2 (2017): 123–37.

Gilman, Sander. *Difference and Pathology: Stereotypes of Sexuality, Race, and Madness.* Ithaca, NY: Cornell University Press, 1985.

Gilman, Sander. *Disease and Representation: Images of Illness from Madness to AIDS*. Ithaca, NY: Cornell University Press, 1988.

Gilman, Sander. *On Blackness without Blacks: Essays on the Image of the Black in Germany*. Boston, MA: G. K. Hall, 1982.

Gilman, Sander. *Picturing Health and Illness: Images of Identity and Difference*. Baltimore, MD: Johns Hopkins University Press, 1995.

Gilroy, Paul. *Postcolonial Melancholia (The Wellek Library Lectures)*. New York: Columbia University Press, 2006.

Goines, Donald. *Crime Partners*. Los Angeles, CA: Holloway House, 1978.

Goines, Donald. *Death List*. Los Angeles, CA: Holloway House, 1974.

Goines, Donald. *Kenyatta's Escape*. Los Angeles, CA: Holloway House, 1974.

Goines, Donald. *Kenyatta's Last Hit*. Los Angeles, CA: Holloway House, 1975.

Gordon, Lewis. "Race, Theodicy and the Normative Emancipatory Challenges of Blackness." *South Atlantic Quarterly* 112, no. 4 (2013): 725–36.

Gorman, Rachel. "Quagmires of Affect: Madness, Labor, Whiteness, and Ideological Disavowal." *American Quarterly* 69, no. 2 (2017): 309–14.

Govan, Sandra. "Connections, Links, and Extended Networks in Octavia Butler's Science Fiction." *Black American Literature Forum* 18, no. 2 (1984): 43–48.

Grimké, Angelina Weld. *Rachel*. Boston, MA: Cornhill, 1920.

Grosz, Elizabeth. *Volatile Bodies: Toward a Corporeal Feminism*. Indianapolis: University of Indiana Press, 1994.

Grusin, Richard, ed. *The Nonhuman Turn*. Minneapolis: University of Minnesota Press, 2015.

Hampton, Gregory Jerome. *Changing Bodies in the Fiction of Octavia Butler: Slaves, Aliens, Vampires*. New York: Lexington Books, 2010.

Haraway, Donna. *Simians, Cyborgs, and Women: The Reinvention of Nature*. New York: Routledge, 1991.

Harb, Siréne. Review of *New Body Politics: Narrating Arab and Black Identity in the Contemporary United States* by Therí A. Pickens. *African American Review* 50, no. 2 (2017): 243–44.

Hartman, Saidiya V. *Lose Your Mother: A Journey along the Atlantic Slave Route*. New York: Farrar, Straus, and Giroux, 2008.

Hartman, Saidiya V. *Scenes of Subjection: Terror, Slavery, and Self-Making in Nineteenth-Century America*. New York: Oxford University Press, 1997.

Hilton, Leon J. "Avonte's Law: Autism, Wandering, and the Racial Surveillance of Neurological Difference." *Blackness and Disability*. Edited by Therí A. Pickens. Special issue, *African American Review* 50, no. 2 (2017): 221–35.

Hine, Darlene Clark. "Rape and the Inner Lives of Black Women in the Middle West." *Signs* 14, no. 4 (1989): 912–20.

Hinton, Anna. "'And So I Bust Back': Violence, Race, and Disability in Hip Hop." *CLA Journal*. 60, no. 3 (2017): 290–304.

Holland, Sharon P. *Erotic Life of Racism*. Durham, NC: Duke University Press, 2012.

Hopkins, Pauline. *Of One Blood, Or the Hidden Self*. New York: Washington Square Press, 2004.

Hopkinson, Nalo. *Brown Girl in the Ring.* New York: Warner Books, 1998.

Hopkinson, Nalo. *The Chaos.* New York: Margaret K. McElderry Books, 2012.

Hopkinson, Nalo. "An Interview with Nalo Hopkinson." Interview with Dianne D. Glave. *Callaloo* 26, no. 1 (2003): 146–59. JSTOR, July 1, 2013.

Hopkinson, Nalo. *Midnight Robber.* New York: Grand Central, 2000.

Hopkinson, Nalo. *The New Moon's Arms.* New York: Grand Central, 2007.

Hopkinson, Nalo. *Salt Roads.* New York: Open Road Integrated Media, 2015.

Hopkinson, Nalo. *Sister Mine.* New York: Grand Central, 2013.

Hopkinson, Nalo. *Skin Folk.* New York: Open Road Integrated Media, 2001.

Jack, Jordynn. *Autism and Gender: From Refrigerator Mothers to Computer Geeks.* Urbana: University of Illinois Press, 2014.

Jackson, Jr., John L. *Racial Paranoia: The Unintended Consequences of Political Correctness.* New York: Civits Books, 2008.

Jackson, Michael. "Wanna Be Startin' Something." *Thriller.* Sony, 1982.

Jackson, Michael. "You Can't Win." *The Wiz.* MCA, 1978.

James, Jennifer. "Gwendolyn Books, World War II and the Politics of Rehabilitation." In *Feminist Disability Studies,* edited by Kim Q. Hall, 136–59. Bloomington: Indiana University Press, 2011.

Jarman, Michelle. "Coming Up from Underground: Uneasy Dialogues at the Intersections of Race, Mental Illness, and Disability Studies." In *Blackness and Disability: Critical Examinations and Cultural Interventions,* edited by Christopher M. Bell, 9–30. East Lansing: Michigan State Press, 2011.

Jarman, Michelle. "Cultural Consumption and Rejection of Precious Jones: Pushing Disability into the Discussion of Sapphire's *Push* and Lee Daniels's *Precious.*" *Feminist Formations* 24, no. 2 (2012): 163–85.

Jarman, Michelle. "Dismembering the Lynch Mob: Intersecting Narratives of Disability, Race, and Sexual Menace." In *Sex and Disability,* edited by Robert McRuer and Anna Mollow, 89–107. Durham, NC: Duke University Press, 2012.

Jarman, Michelle. "Narrative Displacement: The Symbolic Burden of Disability in Zora Neale Hurston's *Seraph on the Suwanee.*" In *"The Inside Light": New Critical Essays on Zora Neale Hurston,* edited by D. G. Plant, 127–37. New York: Prager, 2010.

Jarrett, Gene Andrew. *Deans and Truants: Race and Realism in African American Literature.* Philadelphia: University of Pennsylvania Press, 2007.

Jarrett, Gene Andrew. *Representing the Race: A New Political History of African American Literature.* New York: New York University Press, 2011.

Jenkins, Candice. *Private Lives, Proper Relations: Regulating Black Intimacy.* Minneapolis: University of Minnesota Press, 2007.

Johnson, Harriet McBryde. "Should I Have Been Killed at Birth? The Case for My Life." *New York Times Magazine,* February 16, 2003.

Johnson, Mat. *Dark Rain: A New Orleans Story.* New York: Vertigo, 2010.

Johnson, Mat. *Drop.* New York: Bloomsbury, 2001.

Johnson, Mat. "Foreword." In *Contemporary African American Literature: The Liv-*

ing Canon, edited by Shirley Moody-Turner and Lovalerie King, ix–xii. Bloomington: Indiana University Press, 2013.

Johnson, Mat. *The Great Negro Plot: A Tale of Conspiracy and Murder in Eighteenth-Century New York.* New York: Bloomsbury, 2007.

Johnson, Mat. *Hunting in Harlem.* New York: Bloomsbury, 2003.

Johnson, Mat. *Incognegro.* New York: DC Comics, 2008.

Johnson, Mat. *Loving Day.* New York: Spiegel & Grau, 2015.

Johnson, Mat. *Papa Midnite.* New York: DC Comics, 2006.

Johnson, Mat. *Pym.* New York: Spiegel & Grau, 2012.

Johnson, Mat. *Right State.* New York: DC Comics, 2012.

Jonas, Raymond. *The Battle of Adwa: African Victory in the Age of Empire.* Cambridge, MA: Belknap Press, 2011.

Kafer, Alison. "Compulsory Bodies: Reflections on Heterosexuality and Able-Bodiedness." *Journal of Women's History* 15, no. 3 (2003): 77–89.

Kafer, Alison. *Feminist. Queer. Crip.* Bloomington: Indiana University Press, 2013.

Kafer, Alison. Review of *New Body Politics: Narrating Arab and Black Identity in the Contemporary United States* by Therí A. Pickens. *Disability Studies Quarterly* 37, no. 4 (2017) www.dsq-sds.org March 20, 2018.

Kerschbaum, Stephanie. *Toward a New Rhetoric of Difference.* Urbana, IL: National Council of Teachers of English, 2014.

Khrebtan-Höhager, Julia. Review of *New Body Politics: Narrating Arab and Black Identity in the Contemporary United States* by Therí A. Pickens. *Journal of Race and Policy* 12, no. 1 (2016): 59–62.

Kim, Eunjung. *Curative Violence: Rehabilitating Disability, Gender, and Sexuality in Modern Korea.* Durham, NC: Duke University Press, 2017.

Kriegel, Leonard. "Uncle Tom and Tiny Tim: Some Reflections on the Cripple as Negro." *American Scholar* 38 (1969): 412–30. Last modified 2014. www.disabilitymuseum.org.

Lacey, Lauren J. "Octavia E. Butler on Coping with Power in *Parable of the Sower, Parable of the Talents,* and *Fledgling.*" *Critique* 49, no. 4 (2008): 379–94.

Lavender III, Isiah. *Race in Science Fiction.* Bloomington: Indiana University Press, 2011.

Lawrie, Paul R. D. "'Salvaging the Negro': Race, Rehabilitation, and the Body Politic in World War I America, 1917–1924." In *Disability Histories,* edited by Susan Burch and Michael Rembis, 321–44. Urbana: University of Illinois Press, 2014.

Lewis, Bradley. *Depression: Integrating Science, Culture, and Humanities.* New York: Routledge, 2012.

Lipsitz, George. *The Possessive Investment in Whiteness: How White People Profit from Identity Politics.* Philadelphia, PA: Temple University Press, 2006.

Livingston, Julie. *Debility and the Moral Imagination in Botswana.* Bloomington: Indiana University Press, 2005.

Lorde, Audre. *Burst of Light.* New York: Firebrand Books, 1988.

Lorde, Audre. *The Cancer Journals.* San Francisco, CA: Aunt Lute Books, 1980.

Lorde, Audre. *Zami: A New Spelling of My Name*. Berkeley, CA: Ten Speed Press, 1982.

Lyle, Timothy S. "Trying to Scrub that 'Death Pussy' Clean Again: The Pleasures of Domesticating HIV/AIDS in Pearl Cleage's Fiction." *Blackness and Disability*. Edited by Therí A. Pickens. Special issue, *African American Review* 50, no. 2 (2017): 153–68.

McCormick, Stacie. "August Wilson and the Antispectacle of Blackness and Disability in *Fences* and *Two Trains Running*." *CLA Journal* 61, no. 1. 1–2 (2017): 65–83.

McRuer, Robert. *Crip Theory: Cultural Signs of Queerness and Disability*. New York: New York University Press, 2006.

McRuer, Robert. "Submissive and Non-Compliant: The Shock of Gary Fisher." In *Blackness and Disability: Critical Examinations and Cultural Interventions*, edited by Christopher M. Bell, 95–111. Berlin: LIT Verlag, 2011.

Menzies, Robert, Brenda LeFrançois, and Geoffrey Reaume. "Introducing Mad Studies." In *Mad Matters: A Critical Reader in Canadian Mad Studies*, edited by Brenda LeFrançois, Robert Menzies, and Geoffrey Reaume, 1–23. Toronto, CA: Canadian Scholars' Press, 2013.

Metzl, Jonathan. *The Protest Psychosis: How Schizophrenia Became a Black Disease*. Boston, MA: Beacon Press, 2009.

Minich, Julie Avril. *Accessible Citizenships: Disability, Nation, and the Cultural Politics of Greater Mexico*. Philadelphia, PA: Temple University Press, 2013.

Mitchell, David, and Sharon Snyder. *Narrative Prosthesis: Disability and the Dependencies of Discourse*. Ann Arbor: University of Michigan Press, 2001.

Mock, Janet. "#RedefiningRealness." Public conversation, December 3, 2014, Schaeffer Theater, Bates College, Lewiston, ME.

Mollow, Anna. "Unvictimizable: Toward a Fat Black Disability Studies." *Blackness and Disability*. Edited by Therí A. Pickens. Special issue, *African American Review* 50, no. 2 (2017): 105–21.

Mollow, Anna. "'When Black Women Start Going on Prozac': Race, Gender, and Mental Illness in Meri Nana-Ama Danquah's *Willow Weep for Me*." *Race, Ethnicity, Disability, and Literature: Intersections and Interventions*. Edited by Cynthia Wu and Jennifer James. Special issue, *MELUS* 31, no. 3 (2006): 67–99.

Morris, Susana. "Black Girls are from the Future: Afrofuturist Feminism in Octavia E. Butler's *Fledgling*." *Women's Studies Quarterly* 40, no. 3–4 (2012): 146–66.

Morrison, Toni. *Playing in the Dark: Whiteness and the Literary Imagination*. New York: Vintage Books, 1993.

Morrison, Toni. "Recitatif." In *Leaving Home*, edited by Hazel Rochman and Darlene Z. McCampbell, 201–27. New York: HarperCollins, 1997.

Moten, Fred. "Blackness and Nothingness." *South Atlantic Quarterly* 112, no. 4 (2013): 737–80.

Moten, Fred. *In the Break: The Aesthetics of the Black Radical Tradition*. Minneapolis: University of Minnesota Press, 2003.

Mullen, Harryette. *Sleeping with the Dictionary*. Sacramento: University of California Press, 2002.

Muñoz, José Esteban. *Disidentifications: Queers of Color and the Performance of Politics*. Minneapolis: University of Minnesota Press, 1999.

Murray, Stuart. *Representing Autism: Culture, Narrative, Fascination*. Liverpool, UK: Liverpool University Press, 2008.

Neal, Mark Anthony. *Soul Babies: Black Popular Culture and the Post-Soul Aesthetic*. New York: Routledge, 2002.

Nelson, Alondra. "Introduction: Future Texts." *Afrofuturism*. Edited by Alondra Nelson. Special issue, *Social Text* 20, no. 2 (2002): 1–23.

Nelson, Alondra. "'Making the Impossible Possible': An Interview with Nalo Hopkinson." *Afrofuturism*. Edited by Alondra Nelson. Special issue, *Social Text* 20, no. 2 (2002): 97–115.

Nicki, Andrea. "The Abused Mind: Feminist Theory, Psychiatric Disability, and Trauma." *Hypatia* 16, no. 4 (2001): 80–104.

Nielsen, Kim E. *A Disability History of the United States*. Boston, MA: Beacon Press, 2012.

Noll, Steven, and James W. Trent Jr. Introduction to *Mental Retardation in America: A Historical Reader*, edited by Steven Noll and James W. Trent Jr., 1–23. New York: New York University Press, 2004.

Norris, Keenan. "The Satire of John Killens and Mat Johnson." In *Post-Soul Satire: Black Identity after Civil Rights*, edited by Derek C. Maus and James J. Donahue, 175–88. Jackson: University of Mississippi Press, 2014.

Nyong'o, Tavia. *The Amalgamation Waltz: Race, Performance, and the Ruses of Memory*. Minneapolis: University of Minnesota Press, 2009.

Orem, Sarah. "(Un)necessary Procedures: Black Women, Disability, and Work in *Grey's Anatomy*." *Blackness and Disability*. Edited by Therí A. Pickens. Special issue, *African American Review* 50, no. 2 (2017): 169–83.

Paris is Burning. Dir. Jennie Livingston. Perf. Dorian Corey, André Christian, Carmen and Brooke. Lionsgate, 2012.

Parker, Morgan. *There Are More Beautiful Things Than Beyoncé*. Portland, OR: Tin House Books, 2017.

Petry, Ann. *The Street*. New York: Houghton Mifflin, 1946.

Pickens, Therí A. "Blue Blackness, Black Blueness: Making Sense of Blackness and Disability." *Blackness and Disability*. Edited by Therí A. Pickens. Special issue, *African American Review* 50, no. 2 (2017): 93–103.

Pickens, Therí A. "'It's a Jungle Out There': Blackness and Disability in *Monk*." *Disability Studies Quarterly* 33, no. 3 (2013). www.dsq-sds.org.

Pickens, Therí A. "Modern Family: Circuits of Transmission among Black and Arab Americans." *Blackness and Relationality: An ACLA Forum*. Edited by Keith Feldman. Special issue, *Comparative Literature* 68, no. 2 (2016): 130–40. DOI: 10.1215/00104124–3507912.

Pickens, Therí A. *New Body Politics: Narrating Arab and Black Identity in the Contemporary United States*. New York: Routledge, 2014.

Pickens, Therí A. "Octavia Butler and the Aesthetics of the Novel." *Feminist Dis-*

ability Studies. Edited by Kim Q. Hall. Special issue, *Hypatia* 30, no. 1 (winter 2015): 167–80. DOI: 10.1111/hypa.12129.

Pickens, Therí A. "Satire, Scholarship and Sanity; or How to Make Mad Professors." In *Negotiating Disability Awareness: Disclosure and Higher Education*, edited by Stephanie L. Kerschbaum, Laura T. Eisenman, and James M. Jones, 243–54. Ann Arbor: University of Michigan Press, 2017.

Pickens, Therí A. "The Verb Is No: Towards a Grammar of Black Women's Anger." *"We Were Not Invented Yesterday": Conversations on Being Black Women in the Academy*. Edited by Janeen Price and Janise Hudson. Special issue, *College Language Association Journal* 60, no. 1 (2017): 14–31.

Pickens, Therí A. "What Drives Work: A Written Performance Piece." *On Being a Professor*. Special issue, *Polymath: An Interdisciplinary Arts and Science Journal* 4, no. 1 (2014): 19–23.

Pickens, Therí A. "'You're Supposed to Be a Tall, Handsome, Fully Grown White Man': Theorizing Race, Gender, and Disability in Octavia Butler's *Fledgling*." *Journal of Literary and Cultural Disability Studies* 9, no. 1 (2014): 33–48.

Popp, Valerie L. "'Eloquent Limbs': D. H. Lawrence and the Aesthetics of Disability." *Journal of Literary and Cultural Disability Studies* 5, no. 1 (2011): 35–52.

Prendergast, Catherine. "On the Rhetorics of Mental Disability." In *Embodied Rhetorics: Disability in Language and Culture*, edited by Cynthia Lewiecki-Wilson and James Wilson, 45–60. Carbondale: Southern Illinois University Press, 2001.

Prendergast, Catherine. "Race: The Absent Presence in Composition Studies." *College Composition and Communication* 50, no. 1 (1998): 36–53.

Price, Margaret. "'Her Pronouns Wax and Wane': Psychosocial Disability, Autobiography, and Counter-Diagnosis." *Journal of Literary & Cultural Disability Studies* 3, no. 1 (2009): 11–33.

Price, Margaret. *Mad at School: Rhetorics of Mental Disability and Academic Life*. Ann Arbor: University of Michigan Press, 2011.

Puar, Jasbir K. "'I Would Rather Be a Cyborg Than a Goddess': Becoming-Intersectional in Assemblage Theory." *philoSOPHIA* 2, no. 1 (2012): 49–66.

Puar, Jasbir K. *Terrorist Assemblages: Homonationalism in Queer Times*. Durham, NC: Duke University Press, 2007.

Quashie, Kevin Everod. *The Sovereignty of Quiet: Beyond Resistance in Black Culture*. New Brunswick, NJ: Rutgers University Press, 2012.

Queen, Khadijah. *Black Peculiar*. Blacksburg, VA: Noemi Press, 2011.

Reid-Pharr, Robert. *Once You Go Black: Choice, Desire, and the Black American Intellectual*. New York: New York University Press, 2007.

Rowden, Terry. *The Songs of Blind Folk: African American Musicians and Cultures of Blindness*. Ann Arbor: University of Michigan Press, 2009.

Samuels, Ellen. *Fantasies of Identification: Disability, Gender, Race*. New York: New York University Press, 2014.

Samuels, Ellen. "My Body, My Closet: Invisible Disability and the Limits of

Coming-Out Discourse." GLQ: A Journal of Lesbian and Gay Studies 9, no. 1–2 (2003): 233–55.

Sass, Louis A. Madness and Modernism: Insanity in the Light of Modern Art Literature and Thought. Cambridge, MA: Harvard University Press, 1994.

Schalk, Sami. "Interpreting Disability Metaphor and Race in Octavia Butler's 'The Evening and the Morning and the Night.'" Blackness and Disability. Edited by Therí A. Pickens. Special issue, African American Review 50, no. 2 (2017): 139–51.

Scott, Darieck. Extravagant Abjection: Blackness, Power, and Sexuality in the African American Literary Imagination. New York: New York University Press, 2010.

Senier, Siobhan. "'Traditionally, Disability Was Not Seen as Such': Writing and Healing in the Work of Mohegan Medicine People." Journal of Literary and Cultural Disability Studies 7, no. 2 (2013): 213–29.

Sexton, Jared. Amalgamation Schemes: Antiblackness and the Critique of Multiracialism. Minneapolis: University of Minnesota Press, 2008.

Sexton, Jared. "The Social Life of Social Death: On Afropessimism and Black Optimism." InTensions 5 (2011): 1–47.

Sharpe, Christina. In the Wake: On Blackness and Being. Durham, NC: Duke University Press, 2016.

Sharpe, Christina. Monstrous Intimacies: Making Post Slavery Subjects. Durham, NC: Duke University Press, 2010.

Shockley, Evie. the new black. Middletown, CT: Wesleyan University Press, 2011.

Siebers, Tobin. Disability Theory. Ann Arbor: University of Michigan Press, 2008.

Simplican, Stacey Clifford. The Capacity Contract: Intellectual Disability and the Question of Citizenship. Minneapolis: University of Minnesota Press, 2015.

Smith, Barbara. "Toward a Black Feminist Criticism." In All the Women Are White, All the Blacks Are Men, but Some of Us Are Brave, edited by Gloria Hull, Patricia Bell Scott, and Barbara Smith, 157–75. New York: Feminist Press, 1982.

Smith, Darryl. "Handi-/Cappin' Slaves and Laughter by the Dozens: Divine Dismemberment and Disability Humor in the US." Journal of Literary and Cultural Disability Studies 7, no. 3 (2013): 289–301.

Smith, Eric D. Globalization, Utopia, and Postcolonial Science Fiction. New York: Palgrave McMillan, 2012.

Smith, Valerie. "'Loopholes of Retreat.' Architecture and Ideology in Harriet Jacobs's Incidents in the Life of a Slave Girl." In Reading Black, Reading Feminist, edited by Henry Louis Gates, Jr., 212–26. New York: Plume, 1990.

Snyder, Sharon, and David T. Mitchell. Cultural Locations of Disability. Chicago, IL: University of Chicago Press, 2006.

Sontag, Susan. Illness as Metaphor and AIDS and Its Metaphors. New York: Farrar, Straus, and Giroux, 2013.

Spillers, Hortense J. Black, White, and in Color: Essays on American Literature and Culture. Chicago, IL: University of Chicago Press, 2013.

Spillers, Hortense J. "Interstices: A Drama of Small Words." In Pleasure and Danger: Exploring Female Sexuality, edited by Carol Vance, 73–101. London: Routledge, 1984.

Spillers, Hortense J. "'Mama's Baby, Papa's Maybe': An American Grammar Book." *Diacritics* 17, no. 2 (1987): 65–81.

Suvin, Darko. *Metamorphoses of Science Fiction: On the Poetics and History of a Literary Genre*. New Haven, CT: Yale University Press, 1979.

Suvin, Darko. "The SF Novel in 1969." In *Nebula Award Stories "Five,"* edited by James Blish, 155–65. New York: Doubleday, 1970.

Tettenborn, Éva. "Melancholia as Resistance in Contemporary African American Literature." *Race, Ethnicity, Disability, and Literature: Intersections and Interventions*. Edited by Cynthia Wu and Jennifer James. Special issue, *MELUS* 31, no. 3 (2006): 101–21.

Thomson, Rosemarie Garland. *Extraordinary Bodies: Figuring Physical Disability in American Culture and Literature*. New York: Columbia University Press, 1997.

Thomson, Rosemarie Garland. "Misfits: A Feminist Materialist Disability Concept." *Hypatia* 26, no. 3 (2011): 591–609.

Thomson, Rosemarie Garland. *Staring: How We Look*. New York: Oxford University Press, 2009.

Titchkosky, Tanya. *Reading and Writing Disability Differently: The Textured Life of Embodiment*. Toronto, ON: University of Toronto Press, 2007.

Travis, Jeremy. *But They All Come Back: Facing the Challenges of Prisoner Reentry*. Washington, DC: Urban Institute Press, 2005.

Trethewey, Natasha. *Thrall*. New York: Houghton Mifflin, 2012.

Tyler, Jr., Dennis. "Jim Crow's Disabilities: Racial Injury, Immobility, and the 'Terrible Handicap' in the Literature of James Weldon Johnson." *Blackness and Disability*. Edited by Therí A. Pickens. Special issue, *African American Review* 50, no. 2 (2017): 185–201.

Vargas, João Costa, and Joy A. James. "Refusing Blackness-as-Victimization: Trayvon Martin and the Black Cyborgs." In *Pursuing Trayvon Martin: Historical Contexts and Contemporary Manifestations of Racial Dynamics*, edited by George Yancy and Janine Jones, 193–204. New York: Lexington Books, 2013.

Vedere, Sukshma. Review of *New Body Politics: Narrating Arab and Black Identity in the Contemporary United States* by Therí A. Pickens. *College Language Association Journal* 59, no. 2 (2016): 203–5.

Walcott, Rinaldo. "Caribbean Pop Culture in Canada; Or, the Impossibility of Belonging to the Nation." *Small Axe: A Caribbean Journal of Criticism* 5, no. 1 (2001): 123–40.

Walker, Alice. "Beauty: When the Other Dancer Is the Self." *In Search of Our Mothers' Gardens: Prose*. Orlando, FL: Harcourt Brace Jovanovich Publishers, 1983.

Wanzo, Rebecca. *The Suffering Will Not Be Televised: African American Women and Sentimental Political Storytelling*. Albany, NY: SUNY Press, 2009.

Weheliye, Alexander G. "Feenin': Posthuman Voices in Contemporary Black Popular Music." *Afrofuturism*. Edited by Alondra Nelson. Special issue, *Social Text* 20, no. 2 (2002): 21–48.

Weheliye, Alexander G. *Habeas Viscus: Racializing Assemblages, Biopolitics, and*

Black Feminist Theories of the Human. Durham, NC: Duke University Press, 2014.

Wilderson III, Frank B. *Red, White, and Black: Cinema and the Structure of US Antagonisms*. Durham, NC: Duke University Press, 2010.

Wolfe, George. *The Colored Museum*. New York: Grove Press, 1986.

Wolframe, PhebeAnn M. "The Madwoman in the Academy or Revealing the Invisible Straight-Jacket: Theorizing and Teaching Sanism and Sane Privilege." *Disability and Madness*. Edited by Noam Ostrander and Bruce Henderson. Special issue of *Disability Studies Quarterly* 33, no. 1 (2013). www.dsq-sds.org.

Wright, Michelle. *Physics of Blackness: Beyond the Middle Passage Epistemology*. Minneapolis: University of Minnesota Press, 2015.

Wu, Cynthia. *Chang and Eng Reconnected: The Original Siamese Twins in American Culture*. Philadelphia, PA: Temple University Press, 2012.

Wu, Cynthia, and Jennifer James, eds. "Race, Ethnicity, Disability, and Literature: Intersections and Interventions." Special issue, *MELUS* 31, no. 3 (2006): 3–13.

Wynter, Sylvia. "Africa, the West and the Analogy of Culture: The Cinematic Text after Man." In *Symbolic Narratives / African Cinemas: Audience Theory and Moving Image*, edited by June Givanni, 25–76. London: British Film Institute, 2000.

Wynter, Sylvia. "Unsettling the Coloniality of Being/Power/Truth/Freedom: Towards the Human, after Man, Its Overrepresentation—An Argument." *CR: The New Centennial Review* 3, no. 3 (2003): 257–337.

Yergeau, Melanie. "Aut(hored)ism." *Computers and Composition Online*. (2009). Accessed October 22, 2015. www.cconlinejournal.org/theory.htm.

Yergeau, Melanie. "Clinically Significant Disturbance: On Theorists Who Theorize Theory of Mind." *Disability Studies Quarterly* 33, no. 4 (March 21, 2014). www.dsq-sds.org.

Yergeau, Melanie, et al. "Multimodality in Motion: Disability and Kairotic Space." *Kairos: A Journal of Rhetoric, Technology, and Pedagogy* 18, no. 1 (2013). Accessed 22 October 2015. www.kairos.technorhetoric.net.

Yuan, David. "The Celebrity Freak: Michael Jackson's Grotesque Glory." In *Freakery: Cultural Spectacles of the Extraordinary Body*, edited by Rosemarie Garland Thomson, 368–84. New York: New York University Press, 1996.

invisibility of, 55; language, 116n9; legibility and, 56–57; medicalized notion of, 64; mental illness and, 58–59; in *Midnight Robber*, 59–60, 63; people of color with, 54–55; slaves with, 55; visibility and, 56

cognitive estrangement, 11–12

colonialism: Black culture and, 76–77; Blackness and, 102; language and, 61; postcolonial interpretive strategies, 92–93; postcolonial melancholia, 16; subjugation of human and, 76; transnational, 5

communication, 10, 61

Cooper, Brittney, 18

Crenshaw, Kimberlé, 17–18

cultural narratives, 52

cyborg, 19–20; paradigm, 128n56

Danquah, Meri Nana-Ama, 52–53

Davis, Lennard, 15–16, 50–51, 129n14; *End of Normal*, 7

Debility and the Moral Imagination in Botswana (Livingston), 5

de cardio racism, 83

decolonization, 7

dehumanization, 64

Deleuze, Gilles, 15–16, 18, 28

"Demarginalizing the Intersection of Race and Sex: A Black Feminist Critique of Antidiscrimination Doctrine, Feminist Theory and Antiracist Politics" (Crenshaw), 17–18

depression, 52–53, 116n5

Depression (Lewis), 116n5

disability: abjection and, 80, 90; aesthetics and, 78; in *African Immortals* series, 88–90; agency and, 35; in Black literature, 6, 33; Blackness and, 1–3, 8, 11, 17, 23–25, 29, 52, 80; in Black studies, 9–10; cultures, 52; definitions of, 5; erasure of, 51, 120n2; future and, 49; gender and, 25; iden-

tity and, 97; intellectual, 8; language, 8–9; mutual constitution of race and, 24–29; origins, 62; otherness and, 79; physical, 8; in public sphere, 89; race and, 3, 7, 9, 20–21, 24–25; slavery and, 5, 10; social model of, 32, 122n28; in *The Street*, 33; studies, 7; tropes, 79; value of, 96–97; war and, 35; white-centered notions of, 34; whiteness and, 7

Disability and Difference in Global Contexts (Erevelles), 5

A Disability History of the United States (Nielsen), 27, 121n13

disability studies, 17, 21–22, 62, 95–96; Blackness in, 10; Black studies and, 60; cognitive disability and, 130n26; cyborg and, 19; feminist, 35; future of, 7; human in, 78; madness and, 7–8; mental illness and, 130n26; race and, 23, 115n4, 118n34

Disability Theory (Siebers), 7, 130n25

Donadey, Anne, 86

drapetomania, 8

Du Bois, W. E. B., 53, 109, 123n43

Due, Tananarive, 96; *Blood Colony*, 82, 85–86, 88; *The Living Blood*, 81–82, 87; *My Soul to Keep*, 81, 84; *My Soul to Take*, 82, 88. See also *African Immortals* series

economic utility, cognitive disability and, 56, 63

Elam, Harry, 53–54

End of Normal (Davis), 7

Enlightenment, 75–76, 78, 88

Enlightenment project, 13, 21

epiphenomenal time, 96

Erevelles, Nirmala, 34–35, 55, 80, 88, 126n27; *Disability and Difference in Global Contexts*, 5

erotic, 35

ethnic modernism, 32

Harlem, 99–100, 103–11; mad Black characters of, 98–99, 102–3

Kafer, Alison, 7, 17, 19, 20, 49, 128n2, 128n56; *Feminist. Queer. Crip.*, 130n25
Kindred (Butler), 86, 124n53
Kriegel, Leonard, 1–3

language, 64; ableism and, 65; Black vernacular speech, 51, 125n1, 125n13, 126n23; cognitive disability, 116n9; colonialism and, 61; disability, 8–9; madness, 4, 8; silence and, 61–62
Lavender, Isiah, III, 12
Lewis, Bradley, 116n5
like race analogies, 2–3
linear time, 57–58, 96, 114
Lipsitz, George, 90
literary criticism, 95
The Living Blood (Due), 81–82, 87
Livingston, Julie, 5
logos, 75
Lorde, Audre, 10; *Zami*, 31
Lyle, Timothy S., 123n36
lynch mobs, 27–28

Mad at School: Rhetorics of Mental Disability and Academic Life (Price), 15
mad Blackness, 21, 123n43; in *African Immortals* series, 80–81; erasure of, 66; humanity and, 79–80; in *Hunting in Harlem*, 104; Johnson, M., characters, 99, 102–3; meaning, 95, 109, 112; in *Midnight Robber*, 58–72; narrative and, 57–58, 108
madness: abjection and, 109; in *African Immortals* series, 82–83; behavior and, 45; in Black communities, 72–73; in Black cultural contexts, 51; in Black literature, 14; Blackness and, 3–4, 6; in Black speculative

fiction, 12; cognitive estrangement and, 11–12; definitions of, 4, 117n14; devaluation of, 96; disability studies and, 7–8; discourses, 30; erasure of, 34; euphemisms, 51; experience of, 5; in fiction, 116n5; in Hopkinson, 58; language, 4, 8; racialized, as trope, 53; as social construct, 116n8; sociogenic, 125n8; term, 51; unmaking, 75–76; white, 13. *See also* Black madness; cognitive disability; mental illness
mad studies, 4
McRuer, Robert, 79
medicine in fiction, 116n5
mental illness, 4, 8, 21, 51; in Black communities, 52–53; Blackness and, 26–27; Black women and, 53; citizenship rights and, 121n13; cognitive disability and, 58–59; depression, 52–53, 116n5; disability studies and, 130n26; marginalizing people with, 127n37; public spaces and integration of, 27; statistics, 26–27, 117n14
microaggression, 41–42
Middle Passage, 5–6, 48, 77, 129n9
Midnight Robber (Hopkinson), 21, 52, 58–72; animacy in, 65–66, 68–69; artificial intelligence in, 59, 69–72, 127n56; cognitive disability in, 59–60, 63; folktale in, 71; narrative in, 67, 69, 71; reconciliation narrative in, 67; silence in, 60–61
mind/body binary, 70
Mollow, Anna, 9, 52–53
Morrison, Toni, 11, 14–15, 31, 86
Moten, Fred, 28, 77; *In the Break: The Aesthetics of the Black Radical Tradition*, 16
Mutu, Wangechi, 113
mutual constitution, reading strategy, 24–25, 96; historicizing and, 26–29, 50; recuperation projects and, 25–29, 50; retrieval projects and, 25, 30–35; Samuels on, 26

My Soul to Keep (Due), 81, 84
My Soul to Take (Due), 82, 88

narratives: cultural, 52; mad Blackness and, 57–58, 108; oppressive intracultural, 53. *See also specific works*
Nation of Gods and Earths, 83
neosoul music, 121n18
neuro-diversity, 4
Nielsen, Kim, 27, 121n13
nonhuman, 130n27
novel, genre, 97–98, 132n5; Black, 101–2, 111; Johnson, M., on reading, 100

ocularity, 57–58, 75
oppressive intracultural narratives, 53
otherness, disability and, 79

paranoia, Blackness and, 83
Parker, Morgan, 112
pedophilia, 43–44, 100–101
Petry, Ann, 31–33
physical disability, 8
"Positive Obsession" (Butler), 12–13
postcolonial interpretive strategies, 92–93
postcolonial melancholia, 16
posthuman, 128n3
Price, Margaret, 15
prison industrial complex, 84
Puar, Jasbir, 18
public sphere, 119n44; disabled in, 89; mentally ill in, 27

queer interpretive strategies, 92–93
quotidian, 35

race: ability and, 4, 26, 29; ableism and, 129n11; disability and, 3, 7, 9, 20–21, 24–25; disability studies and, 23, 115n4, 118n34; gender and, 25; like

race analogies, 2–3; mutual constitution of disability and, 24–29; neuro-atypicality and, 8
"The Race for Theory" (Christian), 13
race studies, 7; critical, 95–96
race theory, critical, 7
racialized madness, 53
racialized space, 15–16
racial melancholia, 16
racism: ableism and, 13, 30–31, 36; *de cardio*, 83; in *Fledgling*, 46–47; institutional, 24, 77; systemic, 13; white madness and, 13
Reading and Writing Disability Differently (Titchkosky), 8
recuperating, 26–29, 50
Rehabilitation Act (1973), 2
rememory, 86
resistance, 30–35
retrieval, 30–35
Riding Death in My Sleep (Mutu), 113
Rihanna, 10, 125n7

Samuels, Ellen: *Fantasies of Identification: Disability, Gender, Race*, 25; on mutual constitution, 26
sanity, 15
satire, 111
Schalk, Sami, 6, 9, 98
science fiction genre, 47, 48
sex, interracial, 122n34
sexism, 9
Sexton, Jared Y., 77, 122n34
sexual agency, 40, 42
sexual deviance, 100–101, 132n16
sexuality, 32; in *The Street*, 33
sexual violence, 44, 66
Siebers, Tobin, 78–79, 88; complex embodiment, 19; *Disability Theory*, 7, 130n25
slavery, 63, 84; Blackness and, 102; cognitive disability and, 55; disability and, 5, 10; *drapetomania*, 8

Smith, Valerie, 10
social movements, 2; Black Lives Matter, 119n44
The Sound and the Fury (Faulkner), 28
Spillers, Hortense, 5, 15–16, 28, 120n57
The Street (Petry), 31–33; disability in, 33; internalized ableism in, 33; sexuality in, 33
structural racism, 30, 53
The Suffering Will Not Be Televised (Wanzo), 9
Suvin, Darko, 11
systemic racism, 13

talking book, 10, 70
Thomson, Rosemarie Garland, 75; *Extraordinary Bodies*, 31–32; on Petry, 32–33
time: epiphenomenal, 96; linear, 57–58, 96, 114
Titchkosky, Tanya, 8
transnational borders, 5
tropes: disability, 79; racialized madness, 53
Tubman, Harriet, 89–90
Tyler, Dennis, Jr., 98, 117n19

"Uncle Tom and Tiny Tim: Some Reflections on the Cripple as Negro" (Kriegel), 1–3

Vargas, João Costa, 19–20
violence, 119n42; sexual, 44, 66

Walcott, Rinaldo, 85
Wanzo, Rebecca, 9
war: Black veterans, 56, 57; disability and, 35
Weheliye, Alexander, 48, 120n57
white-centered notions of disability, 34
white liberalism, 34
white madness, 13
whiteness, 15; Blackness and, 32, 122n22; disability and, 7; hegemony of, in literature, 131n45; intersectionality and, 18; possessive investment in, 90
white supremacy, 4, 131n45
Willow Weep for Me: A Black Woman's Journey through Depression, A Memoir (Danquah), 52–53
Wilson, August, 53
Wilson, Darren, 119n44
women of color, 20
Wonder, Stevie, 116n6
Wright, Michelle, 96
Wynter, Sylvia, 76, 79, 120n57

Yergeau, Melanie, 61

Zami (Lorde), 31